BOB BARTON / DAVID BOOTH

# Stories in the Classroom

## STORYTELLING, READING ALOUD AND ROLEPLAYING WITH CHILDREN

Pembroke Publishers Limited

© 1990 Pembroke Publishers Limited
528 Hood Road
Markham, Ontario
L3R 3K9

## Canadian Cataloguing in Publication Data

Barton, Robert, 1939-
   Stories in the classroom

Includes bibliographical references.
ISBN 0-921217-43-9

1. Storytelling. 2. Education, Elementary.
I. Booth, David. II. Title.

LB1042.B37 1990      372.64'2044      C90-093120-5


Published in the U.S.A. by
Heinemann Educational Books, Inc.
70 Court Street
Portsmouth, NH 03801

## Library of Congress Cataloging-in-Publication Data

Barton, Bob.
   Stories in the classroom/Bob Barton and David Booth.
      p.      cm.
   Includes bibliographical references.
   ISBN 0-435-08527-1
   1. Storytelling. 2. Children — Books and reading. 3. Education,
Elementary — Activity programs.     I. Booth, David.     II. Title.
   LB1042.B365      1990
   372.6'42—dc20

                                                           89-77379
                                                           CIP

Editor: David Kilgour
Design: John Zehethofer
Cover Art: Kady MacDonald Denton

Printed and bound in Canada
9  8  7  6  5  4  3  2  1

*For*

*Willa Pauli*

*and*

*William Moore*

## Acknowledgments

We would like to thank our publisher, Mary Macchiusi, for her support over the three-year development of this book; our editor, David Kilgour, for his care and understanding in supporting the book; and the staff of the Children's Book Store, Toronto, for being a constant source of poetry and story for children.

# Contents

# Introduction

*Stories in the Classroom* is our story as teachers over the last thirty years. We began teaching literature and drama in schools with classes on a rotary system, where one group after another would appear in our classrooms every forty minutes. We found our hope and strength in story, stumbling as it were into "storying for a living". To involve our students and to save our lives, we began to explore all the ways and means of having the children work with stories — retelling them, reading them aloud, writing from them, dramatizing them, arguing about them, finding other stories like them, other versions, other authors, and just reading them one more time.

The stories came in all shapes and sizes — novels, tales, legends, picture books, poems, scripts, advertisements — and we grew adept at using a story for all it was worth, both to save our strength and to help the children learn. We had not yet acquired much understanding of why story was so important for children, but it worked in our classrooms and so we continued.

Over the years, the availability of stories for children has increased dramatically, and now we are able to be more selective and adventuresome in choosing the books we use with our children. We welcome the arrival of individualized reading, but somehow we want that time with the whole classroom as a community of learners to remain. Since we moved into working with teachers in in-service and pre-service courses, story has retained its place at the centre of our work.

Now we have dozens of books by informed authorities on why story matters, why we should help children engage in "storying". As well, we can now find stories of all kinds in bookstores for children and in libraries at home, in school, and in the community. Storytellers are now familiar sights at school celebrations.

7

In his postscript to Betty Rosen's book, *And None of It Was Nonsense*, Harold Rosen says:

The impulse to story is present in every child; a storytelling culture in the classroom refines and enlarges upon that impulse.[1]

Our book attempts to address some of the challenges involved in making a "storytelling culture" come to life in the classroom. We specifically set out to address these challenges in terms that would be of use to teachers working with the community of the classroom or groups of children within it. We hope to show:

- how the growth of possibilities for story in the intellects and imaginations of children can be nurtured;
- how children add to their own story hoards the ideas, motifs, values, and language of those they see and listen to;
- how children's own personal stories can add to the fabric of the classroom, thus helping each individual to recognize the value of his/her life experiences, and building in the class a sense of each person's story worth;
- how informal explorations by individuals and small groups can be carried out within the context of the larger community;
- how peer talk can be maximized, rather than funneling all talk through the teacher;
- how children can be encouraged to listen to each other, respond to each other, and build up their responses as a group;
- how the role of the teacher can change from that of "all-knowing sage" to "participant in the exploration".

In the process of building a story culture, we hope to encourage teachers to:
- increase children's awareness of themselves as co-creators of the stories they read and listen to;
- open children's minds to the wonder and the language each story holds;
- foster the cooperative, collaborative, and communal making of stories in every conceivable manner, in a supportive, enriching, and encouraging storying environment.

We want to build a community of storyers, those who create and re-create stories to make new meanings and help structure the events of their own lives.

We can help children to story, to not only use narrative but also see themselves using it — metastorying — as they come to understand the power inherent in story, both in their own stories and in those they will make their own.

From the stone-age Tasaday people of the Philippine rain forest to the suburbanites in Scarsdale, narrative is the only art that exists in all human cultures. It is by narrative that we experience our lives. I would propose that so far from being nonutilitarian, as is often charged, imaginative narrative, which in its refined and printed form we call fiction, was decisive in the creation of our species, and is still essential in the development of each human individual and necessary to the maintenance of his health and pursuit of his purposes.

A person who never develops or who loses his ability to link events and emotions into a conventionally acceptable story is called insane. The inadequate stories he tells are taken as evidence of his insanity. When and if he becomes able to create a normal narrative, he will be judged improving.

So you say that reading a novel is a way to kill time when the real world needs tending to. I tell you that the only world I know is the world as I know it, and I am still learning how to comprehend that. These books are showing me ways of being I could never have managed alone. I am not killing time, I'm trying to make a life.

Kathryn Morton[2]

Story is still at the heart of our classroom teaching, but we are anxious that the children be the storyers, that they develop their story sense, and come to not only experience story but partake in it, working with its inner worlds and outer forms to create ever-increasing circles of meaning. The children are our strength, a community of learners whose members each contribute to the knowledge of others. As we talk together, revealing ideas and attitudes, we alter both others and ourselves. We clarify, modify, magnify the narratives and our ability to create them, and until the children can find themselves in a story, we have not succeeded as teachers who believe in story. We must all be in the story circle and in the story. All at once. All in together. We are the story, all of us.

Bob Barton
David Booth
Toronto
January 1990

# CHAPTER 1

# The Power of Story

NAPOLEON

Children, when was
Napoleon Bonaparte born,
asks teacher.

A thousand years ago, the children say.
A hundred years ago, the children say.
Last year, the children say.
No one knows.

Children, what did
Napoleon Bonaparte do,
asks teacher.

Won a war, the children say.
Lost a war, the children say.
No one knows.

Our butcher had a dog
called Napoleon,
says Frantisek.
The butcher used to beat him and the dog died
of hunger
a year ago.

And all the children are now sorry
for Napoleon.

Miroslav Holub[1]

## Why Children Need Stories

In a colleague's drama classroom, the Grade 7 gifted students entered for their weekly drama class, took their seats quietly, and put their heads on their desks in some strange, silent ritual. The skilled teacher gently probed for the reason for this, and the children revealed that the librarian had completed her reading of *Flowers for Algernon*, and the children, deeply moved, began to question the morality in giving and then taking intelligence from a retarded man. Gradually, the students entered into all aspects of schooling for all types of people, including the problems that arose because of their segregation as "bright" children. The story had become theirs, and they needed to story to put it in perspective, to add it to their story data base. The emotion created by the reading had to be dealt with, processed, understood. The children needed to use their own stories to make sense of the novel.

The drive to story is basic in all human beings. Stories shape our lives and our culture — we cannot live without them.

Stories provide us with a way of seeing into ourselves; they offer us good counsel and can be a source of comfort. Like the incident described in Miroslav Holub's poem "Napoleon", stories connect us to other aspects of life: they put us in touch with larger things like laughter, love, mercy, and compassion. Stories can cause us to raise profound questions and shape the landscape of our minds for the whole of our lives. Author Natalie Babbitt puts it this way:

> More and more I was finding the charm, the excitement, the relief of sliding into the worlds of the stories I read, of escaping my own plain, ordinary life and becoming the hero I was reading about. So while my outer world stayed predictably the same, my inner world grew wider and wider, its possibilities infinite, the choices it suggested for how I *might* live, someday, multiplying with each new story.[2]

The children interviewed by Donald Fry for his book *Children Talk about Books: Seeing Themselves as Readers* indicate in their comments that, for them, stories provide a "living through" experience, not just a "knowing about". It is in stories that they see played out the facts of their own lives that concern them deeply. Says Fry on this point, "We learn from experience in fiction. Stories are not just amusements."[3]

The universal appetite for stories asserts itself long before children can read or write. Storying is an essential element in consciousness — indeed it is part of what it means to be human —

and ultimately quality of living is related to the narrative
that have become available to an individual.

Story is a living context for making meaning. It can reinforce
the imaginative framework of the developing child, give validity to important feelings, promote insights, nourish hope,
reduce anxieties, and provide a rich fantasy life. Story gives
children ways of dealing constructively with inner experience,
communicating an intuitive, subconscious understanding of their
own nature. Being a human being in this world means having
to accept difficult challenges, but it also means encountering wonderful adventures. One task of childhood is to test oneself in
imaginary situations, as Jess Aarons does when he crosses the
bridge to Terabithia.

Carlos Fuentes puts it even more strongly. "One wants to tell
a story, like Scheherazade, in order not to die. It's one of the
oldest urges of mankind. It's a way of stalling death."[4]

Story helps us to gain an understanding of the complexity of
our emotional responses, demonstrated by the expressive voices
of characters speaking eloquently and powerfully of their feelings.
We cannot teach children emotions; we can only help them reveal
them and understand them.

Children must filter their emotional experiences through their
intellects, making sense of all kinds of information, turning story
experiences over and over in their minds, integrating thought
and feeling.

Aidan Chambers says that children can think and feel with
the images that story offers them, storing them in the "museums
of their minds", and classifying them for later use.[5]

Stories do things to people. We know that things happen to
people when they read or hear stories, that any theory about
the place of story in schools has to begin with this fact. Story
is not an exercise in explanation or persuasion but an experience
between the teller and the told.

"Oh Sarah," Ermingard whispered joyfully, "it is like a
story!" "It is a story," said Sarah. "Everything's a story
— I am a story. Miss Minchen is a story."

Frances Hodgson Burnett,
*The Little Princess*[6]

...ap into the universal situations of life, to
...f others in all the world's past, present, and
...ks, suffering, sorrowing, laughing, wondering,
...feeling satisfied but, most of all, tuning into the
...es of all story wisdom.

...nen children enter into story, they are transported to other
worlds, joining in the adventure and the excitement, freed of
their own time and place — and somehow changed by the
experience. They learn about the lives of others and in doing
so develop a better understanding of their own lives.

> . . . the goal of every storyteller consists of fostering in the
> child, at whatever cost, compassion and humanness, this
> miraculous ability of man to be disturbed by another being's
> misfortune, to feel joy about another being's happiness, to
> experience another's fate as your own.
>
> Kornei Chukovsky,
> *From Two To Five*[7]

Story is a continuous process. We borrow from others to see
how our story fits theirs, then we remold it, add to it, alter it,
tell it again anew, always exploring fresh possibilities.

The Tasmanian storyteller Patricia Scott says that our story
has to fit or be made to fit with our experiences, our dreams,
our family's expectations, and those of the community, yet we
can rarely do this without some incongruity.[8] We establish identity in and through our relations with others. Children learn to
read through personal relationships and reading itself becomes
an extension of those relationships. Scott says that other is other,
be it book or mother, casual friend or total environment, and
we relate to that "other" in terms of our particular identities.

We all have our own unique stories, our own ways of storying, our own ways of representing what is, what was, and what
might be. Some of us prefer to live as though each step were
mapped ahead, some seem to prefer hidden paths, some seem
to deliberately confuse any landmarks around them. We need
to be able to explore other people through touch and word,
through glance and laughter, and respond to their cues and have
them respond to ours.

I tell my story. You retell it, with all of your own life

experiences playing upon it, and suddenly it is your story. Then, we tell our two stories to a third member of the story tribe, and he listens to both and builds a new, personalized version that shocks us with its twists and turns. And we are present at the birth of a new story; we now have three for our story bag, and every time I choose one of those to share, I will unknowingly, unwittingly include bits and scraps from all of them and suddenly I am telling a different story, but it is still mine, and the story is inside, outside, and all around my head. Such is membership in the story tribe.

Our second reading of a story is never the same as the first. We have changed and so have our expectations of the story. A Chinese proverb says that you can never step in the same river twice.

When young children listen to stories, they develop the sense of narrative that will be the core of their thinking and languaging processes. The story continum that will last for a lifetime begins in the earliest years, and continues forever. Children who are provided with a rich story environment — both in hearing stories and in talking about them — will grow as thinkers and as storyers.

Consider the language children meet in a story: words they can absorb into their own language data bases; expressions that range from the archaic to the jazziest contemporary slang; patterns that ring in their ears and seduce them into joining in. How much fun it can be to share a good story, to be delighted or surprised by words artfully arranged to create a narrative. Children tune in to the wonders of language, to the power that lies in becoming the one who stories. According to Katherine Paterson:

. . . we must try, always conscious of our own fragmentary knowledge and nature, to give our children these words. I know as you do that words can be used for evil as well as good. But we must take that risk. We must try as best we are able to give our children words that will shape their minds so they can make those miraculous leaps of imagination that no sinless computer will ever be able to rival — those connections in science, in art, in the living of this life that will reveal the little truths. For it is these little truths that point to the awesome, unknowable unity, the Truth, which holds us together and makes us members one of another.[9]

Given the opportunity, children come to know the anatomy of story, its forms, genres, motifs, patterns, universals, words, and images. Story acquaints children (even those who do not or cannot read) with a variety of language patterns, some of which may be outside their language community. It familiarizes them with literary language, an awareness they will need as readers and writers. And the words that are found in story — where else would a child meet them? Words from other times and places, words found only in print, shared by storytellers with magic literary storehouses, idioms, expressions, metaphors, allusions — all to be met and savored, some to be retained in the mind's eye. Children will meet familiar words used in interesting and unusual contexts, words that tumble and scramble and fall, engorged with meanings. We know that as teachers, we need story words for our children, to take them farther than we could alone, to touch them more deeply, and to delight and chill them with language far outside the confines of the classroom.

Going back, way back, to the earliest of times, when men and women and children looked at one another, at the land, at the sky, at rivers and oceans, at mountains and deserts, at animals and plants, and wondered, as it is in our nature to do: what is all this that I see and hear and find unfolding before me? How shall I comprehend the life that is in me and around me? To do so, stories were constructed — and told, and remembered, and handed down over time, over the generations.

Robert Coles,
*The Call of Stories*[10]

What a place to begin — a story. You can enter it at will, look around, run for cover or stay and consider the events in relation to your own world, reconcile the contradictions, contemplate the ideas, the emotions, the events, the relationships. And you can connect it to other people, other times, other selves, other stories.

# Why Children Need to Story

In many book experiences in school, children study a story, answer questions about it, and explain what they like or dislike about it, but seldom do they engage in narrative, in practising the art of storying, in developing their "story sense". This is changing with the emphasis on holistic teaching and process writing, and with having older children share stories with younger children, but we would propose that using narrative as a means of expression and reflection should be the core of the curriculum. We learn to story by storying.

Aidan Chambers says that

> gossip is the most basic form of story-telling. It is the story of our lives told by our tongues in daily episodes, entertaining but trivial. But sometimes gossip possesses a curiously powerful significance that reaches beyond one time and place, and is handed down year after year from person to person, changed a little here, polished a little there. Then it becomes what we now call a folk tale. When this kind of gossip is about God, or gods, it becomes a myth. When it is about the strange, unnatural phenomena of life, it becomes a fairy tale. Gossip in which we try to get into the essence of something, try to concentrate our experience rather than pack it, tends to become poetry — what Auden I think called memorable speech. In one way or another we all tell ourselves and each other stories about life.[11]

And what of our own stories — our daydreams, our gossip, our family anecdotes? We pass the time of day in conversation, talk, chatter, exchanging ideas and stories. We need real opportunities for conversation so that we can order our thoughts.

School life is full of contexts for story making — an oral culture of gossip in the cloakroom, retellings of TV shows, games and songs at recess, anecdotes about what happened on the weekend.

We construct stories from the events in our lives so that we can make sense of them. James Britton has given us a useful way of looking at story's ability to involve and to distance all at once, with his concept of spectator/participant. In the role of participants we take part in the affairs of our lives; as spectators or onlookers, we are freed from the need to act and can

> contemplate what has happened to us or to other people, or what might conceivably happen; in other words, we improvise upon our world representation — and we may do so either to enrich it, to embroider it, to fill in its gaps and extend its frontiers, or to iron out its inconsistencies.[12]

Through story, we can compare the worlds authors create with our own representations, re-evaluate our own feelings and ideas, come to terms with past experiences, enter into the lives of others, and hone our own abilities to predict and anticipate. We can learn through story to become reflective participants and spectators.

Children play out their lives through story. It tells them that life will go on, and gives form to what has happened, what is happening, and what may happen, ordering their experiences through gossip and anecdote and tale. They need stories from us to give reassurance to their inner stories, the ones that demonstrate their curiosities, fears, and concerns.

We are storytelling animals. Story — narrative — exists in all cultures. It shapes the human condition — imagination, thought, and feelings — through the magic of story forms and structures. Much of the emphasis in this book is on paying attention to the meanings which readers and listeners bring to the experience of story. Let us consider for a moment the tellers and writers and what it is they do.

Perhaps one of the most interesting glimpses into the writer's job was described by Valerie Martin in a *New York Times* article, "Waiting For The Story To Start", in which she examined the responses of writers from Virginia Woolf to Joyce Carol Oates, from Margaret Atwood to John Fowles, to the questions: "How do you start your stories?"; "How do you keep them going?"; "What are your life experiences which have impacted upon you?"

What was startling in their responses was their similarity. All of them began with a single image.

Here are John Fowles's published notes on the origin of his novel *The French Lieutenant's Woman*; in them he describes not only how he got started but how the story stayed alive for him, almost insisting on being written:

18

It started four or five months ago as a visual image. A woman stands at the end of a deserted quay and looks out to sea. That was all. This image rose in my mind one morning when I was still in bed half asleep. It responded to no actual incident in my life (or in art) that I can recall, though I have for many years collected obscure books and forgotten prints, all sorts of flotsam and jetsam from the last two or three centuries, relics of past lives — and I suppose this leaves me with a sort of dense hinterland from which such images percolate down to the coast of consciousness.

These mythopoetic 'stills' (they seem almost always static) float into my mind very often. I ignore them, since that is the best way of finding whether they really are the door into a new world.

So I ignored this image; but it recurred. Imperceptibly it stopped coming to me. I began deliberately to recall it and to try to analyze and hypothesize why it held some sort of imminent power. It was obviously mysterious. It was vaguely romantic. It also seemed, perhaps because of the latter quality, not to belong to today. The woman obstinately refused to stare out of the window of an airport lounge; it had to be this ancient quay — as I happen to live near one, so near that I can see it from the bottom of my garden, it soon became a specific ancient quay. The woman had no face, no particular degree of sexuality. But she was Victorian; and since I always saw her in the same static long shot, with her back turned, she represented a reproach on the Victorian age. An outcast. I didn't know her crime, but I wished to protect her. That is, I began to fall in love with her. Or with her stance. I didn't know which.

The importance of this, comments Martin, has to do with the basic necessity of all stories — *they must engage the senses of the reader*: "it is the engagement, sudden, unexpected and complete, of our senses that moves us in reality as well as fiction."

The desire at the start is not to say anything, not to make meaning, but to create for the unwary reader a sudden experience of reality.

For the would-be writer, Martin advises, "open eyes and ears, take off the blinders . . . let the images pour in and there's one other thing — a sense of free play is required."[13]

Author Jean Little gives us a pretty good idea about a sense of free play in the preface to her book *Hey World, Here I Am:*

MY INTRODUCTION TO KATE

I first met Kate Bloomfield when she walked into a book I was writing. The book was later published by Harper and Row under the title *Look through My Window*. It is about a girl called Emily Blair and, when Kate arrived the evening before school began and stood in the shadows of Emily's lawn, I thought she was just another minor character. I also imagined that I had created her and would remain in control of her. I had a lot to learn about Kate.

Since that first meeting, she, with the strong support of my editor Ellen Rudin, made me turn two mansucripts into one novel, with herself anything but a minor character. I so enjoyed writing her poems in *Look through My Window* that she gave me the privilege of writing down lots more of them as she thought them up. This led to her persuading me to write, at her dictation, the first draft of another book-length manuscript. That took us three days! It was in the first person and she called it *Kate*. Then she left me, except for dropping by to criticize, while I spent a year rewriting it. *Kate* was also published by Harper and Row. You'd think that would satisfy her. Not my Kate! Now she has me aiding and abetting her in having her poems published in this separate volume.

I love Kate, which is why I give in to her so often. Yet the strange thing about our relationship is that, while I know her almost as well as I know myself, she is Emily's friend, not mine, and she lives in a world I write about and watch but cannot enter. I tell myself that her world would not exist if it were not for me. After all, her poems are written down in MY handwriting. They are written from her point of view but I think up the words. Yet I have this eerie feeling that Kate might have found somebody else to write her poetry down for her if I hadn't been around. I am often asked if the characters in my books are "real." My answer is, "They seem more real, to me, than you are." This is particularly true of Kate.

Some of the poems in this collection appeared earlier in my novels *Look through My Window* and *Kate*. If you have read them there, you may notice that certain words or phrases have been changed. Kate is a true writer. She revises her work as she matures. Her poems are dashed down as fast as I can write, in the beginning; but, afterwards, she and I read them over and polish them. A few turned out to be trash, when we reread them. We threw those away. Some we like have had to be omitted because including them would have made the book too long.

Since these poems are a combined effort, Kate and I are sharing equally in dedicating them to the two people whose friendship brought them into being.[14]

It is just this kind of experience that Martin claims critics and students have so much difficulty understanding:

Their notion is that writers and storytellers set out to create something "meaningful", and that to do so they must lace the work with clues to its meaning, usually symbols that have to do with colors or nature, the location of a river or a train track. Many students (and teachers) want to believe that storytelling — whether spoken or written — is a kind of craft, a superior form of cooking or tapestry weaving, in which the teller is in total control from start to finish. No amount of denial is sufficient to obviate this notion.

Perhaps this widespread belief is caused by the fact that good stories just don't seem to be accidental. They look meaningful; they contain symbolic patterns; you can take them apart and find pieces that fit right back together again. They are organic, like flowers; they have an internal and external structure. In fact, like the hands that deal them out, they show their cards now and then; they appear to have a subconscious as well as a conscious level.

Stories think, and they do it in the same way we do. They talk straight sometimes, right to the heart, but they have always a deep, symbolic understanding of reality that can dictate what happens on a conscious level. This analogy to our thinking may explain why stories are so important to us and why they appear to be so meaningful. They speak to us, as dreams speak to us, in a language that is at once highly symbolic and childishly literal. They mirror our consciousness exactly because they are composed through a process both conscious and subconscious.

Certainly, Martin points out some important clues for teachers in their work with children. Pay attention to the story, let its images pour through, and talk about them. And trust the story to do its work.

Stories do not offer single meanings, but form sets of meanings; listening to a story is a search for these meanings through the meanings we already possess. For this reason, encouraging the retelling of stories puts children in a classroom in touch with many perspectives on stories and affords opportunity to think deeply about their implications as well as to realize that listening and reading are continuous transactions between an audience and a story.

We know children have stories before they come to school, family stories that are told over and over again. As teachers, we can tap into these home tales and home truths, and use them to connect with other stories from other families in other times in other worlds. Teachers can also share personal stories from their own lives, engaging in the storying process as both spectators and participants. We must value the family stories, the recess rhymes, the urban rumors, the tall tales; they are gold spun into story and they add to our wealth as storyers. But perhaps it is our hopes of making children strong with written stories as well, authored tales that involve the reading and writing processes, that drive us into focusing on books rather than on stories, on reading instead of on storying, on "reading comprehension" when meaning or understanding should be the outcome. How can we put literacy in place without damaging the story flowers?

## Story Goes to School

My mother read to me from the time I was a baby, and once, when I was three or four and she was reading my favorite story, the words on the page, her spoken words, and the scenes in my head fell together in a blinding flash. I could read!

The story was "Little Red Riding Hood," and it was so much a part of me that I actually became Little Red Riding Hood. My mother sewed me a red satin cape with a hood that I wore almost every day, and on those days, she would make me a "basket of goodies" to take to my grandmother's house. (My only grandmother lived in Rhode Island, three hundred miles away, but that didn't matter.) I'd take the basket and carefully negotiate the backyard, "going to Grandmother's house." My dog, Tippy, was the wolf. Whenever we met, which in a small backyard had to be fairly often, there was an intense confrontation.

Trina Shart Hyman,
*Once Upon a Time*[15]

There has been increasing evidence presented in volumes of research over the past few years that confirms that children who come from homes where reading aloud is a daily occurrence and where books and talk are plentiful, anticipate learning to read with pleasure and indeed often turn up at school already able to do so, while children who have not had this experience are often the ones who find learning to read difficult.

In such instances, sharing stories with children is crucial in order to take up the slack, but it's also essential to continue the practice with those for whom it is already established.

Reading, telling stories and poems, and sharing picture books are major planks in early reading programs at school. Such activities must continue to enrich the language arts program throughout the elementary and secondary years.

It is possible to do so much with stories. They can be burrowed into, built onto; they can provide the stimuli for talk, extended reading, and a host of interpretive activities.

As teachers, we need to help children build connections between their experiences and the sense they make of those experiences, through encouraging them to story with their own stories and the stories of others. It is this connection between the child's own story world and the print world of school that worries us the most. We must not diminish the storying power of children with print.

For many children, and we might say most, schools are the central means of their meeting print stories face to face, and as teachers we feel responsible for how the children will feel about the stories and experiences they find in our classrooms. We must take care to build, not demand, a story community, to leave the children with words and images and ideas to seed their imaginations.

Literary story is missing in the lives of many children. Aside from television's passive, non-interactive storying, some children hear no stories read or told until they go to school. With broken families, crowded schedules, new curricula, and urban development, comes the tragedy of children without stories. Grandparents who might have told stories may be unavailable or live far away; the home may not be a storying place; books may be foreign objects; television may dominate the home and destroy talk-time; parents may be shift workers; single parents may lack time and energy for sharing story; crowded homes may lack quiet places for reading aloud; storytelling may not be considered a significant experience by the adults in the home.

It may be that school will have to bear the burden of story on its shoulders, that teachers will be the storytellers who reach most children. And yet with the burden come the related strengths that accompany story in school: curriculum connection; embedded literacy situations; tribal circles of shared experience; modeling of story strength by adults; the narrative power that each child will acquire from schooling and learning; a sensitivity to authors and illustrators, along with a recognition that the child belongs in this authoring relationship; a wide range of story content, chosen to broaden the child's experiential background, and inclusion of a body of story that carefully and subtly looks at issues of identity, community, sex, race, culture, and so on, and constitutes an exploration of genres and modes of writing that may be unavailable to a child at home; books by a diversity of authors, North American, South American, Australian, New Zealand, European, African and Asian, male and female, old and young, books out of print, books hot off the press.

Access to story becomes vital to a teacher's success with story.

Bookstores that specialize in children's books, libraries within the school and community, conferences where new books are displayed, guest authors and storytellers, books about books written for teachers and parents, books on video and film, tape, and record, books that the teacher loved as a child, books that surprise and shock her into reading . . . all these possibilities must be followed if a classroom is to be story-rich, not story-poor.

A teacher came into one academic's office and gasped at the books on the shelves, on the floor, on the desk. She said that she had found a fairyland for children and teachers. When asked about books in her classroom, she replied that she taught "special ed" and that there was no money in her specialty for such things. And yet her students may be the children who have most need of story entertainment — children who are afraid of print, or who are preliterate or with another language as their native tongue, children for whom story has not been a natural acquisition. The lure of skill sheets for unskilled readers is strong, but what we need are language experiences that open up story and release print power. Children who have not as yet been awakened to literacy must be drawn to it, so that they feel that they want it and need it. They need all kinds of experiences with books: at home; in the classroom; in school and in public libraries; and in book clubs and bookstores. They must develop an ease with story and with all print, so that difficulties do not deter them from the meaning for which they are searching. They must become people who see print as always possible, and who feel comfortable with narrative patterns that lead them to associate story with learning and satisfaction. School and story can be partners in developing the potential of children. If stories do not touch a child in some way, then their strength will not become part of that child's life. Lifeless stories, stories written to convey messages, stories with stereotyped situations or people, stories too far away from the child's experience — these stories do not affect the child, except in a negative way. Good stories enrich and extend all types of knowledge, and become patterns and ideas for future learning.

The sharing of stories presents a variety of models for children. They hear and read stories with powerful and imaginative language and structures; they observe skilled readers and storytellers building moods and weaving spells; they listen and react to other children discussing and creating interpretations.

Kieran Egan presents an interesting model that connects all teaching to storytelling. He suggests that teachers could draw upon the power of the story form, a cultural universe, to teach any content, meaningfully and engagingly, using children's imaginations. He then designs a model of teaching that draws upon the power of the story form for embedding information in an abstract context (story) that everyone already understands. Teaching should use the story model, for "stories are wonderful tools for efficiently organizing and communicating meaning."[16]

In our own teaching, we have attempted to choose stories carefully, and to provide as many story-based classroom activities as possible. Our true work lies in helping children experience story, opening up to them all possible responses as the only authentic means of understanding all forms of story — and all forms of print.

Children enjoy stories. They sense the freedom in the structure, the elixir in the container. They begin to anticipate and predict from the first moments of a story's beginning. They gather round the storyer and know that the experience will be worthwhile. There will be learning, but first there will be story, and the initial responses of children will be personal and organic. Good teachers will move children on to other learning areas, focusing the experience as the children are caught up in all of the ideas being explored. But we must be careful not to use stories solely for our own teaching goals. Story is an art-form unto itself, a worthwhile experience without teaching follow-ups. If we can enrich and extend learning with story, so much the better.

In classrooms where children are exposed to a wide range of stories and books and where they are encouraged to think of themselves as authors too, the functions of reading quickly become apparent. When this kind of reading experience is reinforced through collaboration between home and school with respect to shared reading experiences, opportunities to help children know stories more fully and like them better are greatly enhanced.

As teachers, we care about the stories we use, and we realize the powerful effect of narrative on children. When they hear the story we read or tell, they listen to the heartbeats of those beside them in the story circle. They are the storyteller, the story, and the listener, all in one.

We have seen teachers of all types sharing stories — first-time student teachers, teachers with forty years' experience, teachers with voice training from Royal Academies, teachers who could hardly be heard, teachers who had never heard a story told, teachers who read what their teachers had read, teachers too tired to stand, teachers wearing a storytelling apron, teachers drawing children into a tale, teachers reading from the safety of a lectern, teachers who found a story accidentally, teachers with libraries that would shame us — and in every case, if the story was given honestly, with belief and commitment, the children listened, and often begged for more. Whenever a principal entered our classrooms years ago and caught us reading to the class, we would grow embarrassed or defensive; now we invite the administration in to listen, to laugh, to join in, even to share a story of his or her own. Such are the changes in our lives since story went to school. Dick, Jane, Puff, Spot, and Baby Sally have been rescued by truth, tears, laughter, and empathy. Mother has been freed from scrubbing the floor in her good dress, and Father has abandoned his tie and his fedora. Story is here, and it is powerful.

The challenges in bringing about a story culture in the classroom are many, but so are the strategies. We will deal with these strategies in detail later, but here is a taste of what you and your class can do.

Initially, the cumulative and chain patterns of stories from the oral tradition can be explored. Oral storytelling which invites chiming in draws children naturally into an awareness of patterns. In composing together or alone, these patterns can lead to much experimenting with writing.

Picture books can employ two modes of narration simultaneously. For example, in Vera and Jennifer Williams's *Stringbean's Journey to the Sea*, picture postcards tell a story of the land and its highlights while the messages on the back of the postcards counterpoint the visual and tell the emotional and human side of the story.

Many children's books succeed as parodies of specific tales, tale types, or genres. *The Wild Washerwomen*, by John Yeoman, with illustrations by Quentin Blake, is just such a tale. In a "Seven Brides for Seven Brothers" spoof, this feminist rendering illustrates how writers can break rules to achieve the desired effect.

Texts inside other texts are another pattern children can spot as their own story repertoire grows. Janet and Allan Ahlberg have been immensely successful at integrating familiar texts into new ones — *Each Peach Pear Plum* and *The Jolly Postman*, for example.

Strip cartoon stories such as Raymond Briggs's *Snowman* are rich in ideas for storytelling. Asides, private thoughts, and flashbacks, all done visually, model how to read the story.

Teachers can help children to read particular kinds of texts. Highly predictable books, including traditional tales, nursery rhymes, ABCs, poetry, and pop-up books, form the groundwork for future exploration of folk and fairy tales, fantasy and science fiction, myth and legend.

Once children are familiar with these categories, they have a vocabulary with which to compare and gauge many of the works they will encounter.

Australian educator Maurice Saxby makes this important point:

> I have listened to children discuss with sympathetic insight how the fear of failure forced John Sager to bully his sibling every step of the way in *Children on the Oregon Trail*; how the proud independence of Karana in *Island of the Blue Dolphins* was necessary to her survival; how Ingeborg draws upon her Lapp heritage for her victory in *When Jays Fly to Barbmo*; and how in *Julie of the Wolves* Julie faces squarely the tensions between the old and the new in the Eskimo tradition. These same children used their insights to scrutinize their own behaviour and examine their value system. Thus literature does its own work.[17]

The sharing of stories with children has been a life mission for author Bill Martin, Jr. For him, stories are the most effective means of establishing that "great lifeline known as rapport."[18] If we wish to interest children in education we must make it interesting, and not only do stories help to develop positive attitudes towards teachers and towards school, they also provide a rich source of ideas around which minds can come together. If we want children to make words work for them, then we must surely be prepared to demonstrate that words can work in pleasurable ways.

What can a story do for a particular curriculum area? Consider in social science a topic such as the pioneer or immigrant. While some children copy blackboard notes, others are reading *Sarah Plain and Tall* or *Brothers of the Heart*, or listening to the teacher reading Ann Turner's *Dakota Dugout*, in which a grandmother tells her granddaughter what it was like to live in a sod house on the Dakota prairie a century ago.

Perhaps Turner's book *Heron Street*, about the encroachment of humans on nature as civilization sweeps across the country, would give children a sense of history, or *Anno's Journey* by Mitsumasa Anno, in which a character first appears on the page alone, and then on each new page the same land area is pictured as the town grows through trade and commerce, until he leaves alone on the last page. The story of history can and should be told through art, through story and song, so that the feelings of those who were here before us are part of our interpretation of the past.

STORY QUESTIONS FOR CHILDREN
AND THEIR TEACHERS

Did the story happen to me?
Did I borrow the story?
Should I borrow the story?
Can I put myself in your story?
(Will you know my presence there?)
Is it my story when you write it?
Is it my story if I read yours?
Can two people own a story?
Can anyone own a story?
Are there stories I shouldn't hear?
Are there stories I shouldn't tell?
Did I dream my story?
Did you dream the same one?
Will you read me a story?
Will you tell me a story?
If you do, is the story yours?
Does it become mine in the sharing?

If I tell the story, whose words should I
  use?
Will you listen?
Will you join in the telling?
Shall we sing the story?
Shall we paint the story?
Shall we dance the story?
Shall we be the story?
Can you find another story like this one?
Where did you find it?
May I have it?
May I tell it?
Did the story happen to me?
Am I the story?

CHAPTER **2**

# The Story Tribe

MOUTH OPEN STORY JUMP OUT

Mouth open
story jump out

I tell you me secret
you let it out

But I don't care
if the world hear
shout it out

Mouth open
story jump out

Besides,
the secret I tell you
wasn't even true
so you can shout
till you blue

So boo
mouth open
story jump out

John Agard[1]

## A Storying Community

The oral tradition — stories told aloud — goes right back to the tribe and its communal life. When children become a community of listeners, they lay aside their own egocentricity, and become a tribe.

The whole tribal story experience is composed of each individual's contributions and these must be met with both acceptance and respect. Betty Rosen says that working with a story must be a "shared, mutually supportive concern.

31

The communal spirit accentuates the individuality of its members."[2]

As story sharers, we become all the voices we have ever heard. Each story releases the natural rhythms of language and emotion in us, and sophisticated varieties of style and originality are within each individual's abilities, at least over a period of time.

Many of our encounters with written stories — literature — in school are shaped by our experiences with those who are sharing the stories with us. There is a triangle formed by the children, the story, and the teacher. In the past, our belief as teachers often lay in helping children find "The Truth" hidden in the text, but now we realize that in order to understand a story we must negotiate the meaning between the reader and the author. There occurs a dynamic reading transaction, where students begin to trust their own responses — thoughts and feelings — and then explore and share these with others.

Every time we read a story, it is created anew. We see that story from our own perspectives, using our experiences to make new sense of that story. We now see reading as a co-creative or re-creative act. As we retell a story, we resynthesize and restate ourselves, in our present versions. By being involved in the reading experiences of others, we learn to look at our own subjective responses with some objectivity. We begin to recognize our own styles of perception, exploring others' methods of making texts mean something. Insightful and skilled teachers give young readers help in building imaginative re-creations, retelling stories in a variety of ways. Each story is raw material for children as they explore the range of possibilities in shaping their own personal and collective responses. As teachers, we must be careful to understand the sensitivity and imagination that children bring to a text, and to understand the suggestivity of a story in creating imaginative responses.

We must help children find the voice of a story and explore ways to help that voice speak aloud. Readers are important people in determining what that voice becomes and what it stands for. Although we read many books alone, we still meet together in company to share texts. While each reader brings to a story a different set of life experiences, shared retellings and re-creations affect each individual's perception of the story he or she is building and adds to the patina of the text. Through story, we live through an experience that we have not actually had, but we make sense of it by comparing it with our own lives, our own living.

Some story worlds are easy for us to enter: we have seen that mountain, we have lived in that city, we have known those bulrushes, or we have owned a dog like the one in the story. Other stories are more difficult to enter: we need the artful author who invites us in, the clever storyteller who pulls us along, or the insightful teacher who builds us a shared context. As we hear or read the words, we create a set of images in our minds, we transform those symbols into startling pictures that let us see into the story.

Wolfgang Iser says that the author and reader are to share the game of the imagination, and indeed the game will not work if the text sets out to be anything more than a set of governing rules. Children build up their impressions of a story as they go along "from a moving viewpoint which travels along inside that which it has to apprehend."[3] This wandering viewpoint allows the reader to add to the possibilities that lie within this transactional mode of creation. All readers are making some kinds of meanings through their interactions: who are we to judge which are "correct"? There must be no elitism in teaching. It is this dynamic of the act of reading, the act of storying, that will allow teachers to help individual students with their own transactions with the text. As we combine literary and lived-through experiences, we make meaning of each story, and by sharing our collective meanings, we build our own stronger and bigger world. We must reassure students of the validity of their own personal reconstructions. Shared story experiences may help children to come to know how they read, and how they listen, and how they make meaning, what their own personal perspective is. As Margaret Meek says, we extend each other's seeing through a series of collaborative explorations, allowing for revisitings and reflections of a primarily personal nature.[4]

In the classroom, the teacher is the one who shares a story by reading it aloud, by telling it, by having the children join in, by inviting guests to bring the stories, either in person or on tape. (Do not think we have forgotten the children as storymakers. We will deal with their story adventures in a later chapter.) We do not like the idea of having young people present a memorized tale or recite a complicated narrative, or of asking an audience to sit through a story experience that is lacking in interpretive power or feeling. We will demonstrate a myriad of activities to help children story, but our first strategy is to have adults in the classroom who select and share stories from all cultures for all children, who take the class places they could not go without us. If we can carry the stories to the children, they will welcome us, join us, and story alongside us; they will join the tribe.

We choose a story to read to children every time we meet them — daily or even more frequently — and we select stories that are suitable for the village square. We try to find stories that touch children of different ages, experiences, and abilities in different ways; the closeness of the class often helps everyone to find meaning in the story being shared aloud. We tend not to read to them what they read for themselves, or what they will read for themselves in the future. We choose a variety of story types and themes, stories that will affect them, surprise them, make them laugh, make them wonder, stories that model in their very being the strength of narrative. We enjoy sharing different versions of the same tale, perhaps a retelling with powerful illustrations, a story from an unfamiliar culture, a story from a time far from that of our students, a story that stands on the shoulders of other stories they may have met.

When we share stories that we believe in and enjoy, as members of the group, we are building a context for story, an opportunity for the children to become connected, to become members of the story community.

When we share stories together, we learn how others read. We learn how others respond by what questions they have in their heads, what approaches to story they use. We come to understand the variations in response, we come to appreciate the importance of participating in order to make more meaning.

We want to preserve the sense of shared experience that arises from the range of individual responses. We want to set up, as Harold Rosen says, "classroom situations where pupils have plenty to say and where they feel easy about saying it."[5]

There can be no more dynamic means at a teacher's disposal for bridging the universality of human experience contained in stories and books on the one hand, and a child's limited experiences and reading skills on the other, than sharing stories aloud.

The coming together to hear stimulating material presented by an enthusiastic teller or reader resembles a ritual initiation which reinforces the idea that each and every human being is part of the total interconnectedness of things.

By listening to intonation, pause, pitch, rhetoric, and the sympathetic response of the human voice to the rhythms of language, children are extended well beyond their personal reading capacity. Listening, children quickly build a story repertoire which, if it becomes the stuff of their reading, is like visiting old friends. Simultaneously they come to understand what to expect of a story's structural pattern, conventions, and connection to the world of storytelling. But most important is what author Julius Lester states so succinctly:

> For all the conveniences and new efficiencies technology brings into our lives, it does not have the power to touch us in that solitary place where we all live. It does not have the capacity to link our solitary souls like pearls on a string, bringing us together into a shared and luminous humanity.[6]

The oral tradition lives in stories that adults tell and read to children. A strong narrative line draws children into the experience and helps them along in the story journey. Since they are hearing the narrative, they are able to understand words, ideas, customs, and values that lie outside their reading abilities. Sharing stories with children allows them to enter worlds past, present, and future, to experience life through the ear, and to absorb print in an interesting, non-threatening, and significant manner. Listening to stories told or read aloud gives children their future strength in reading.

Sometimes adults forget that children in the middle years especially need to hear stories read aloud. Through modeling, adults demonstrate the importance of reading, the attitude towards print, and the satisfaction of story, and share literary selections, styles, and vocabulary that may be absorbed by children. By choosing books that children themselves may not, or by selecting stories from other countries and cultures, adults bring a sophisticated, multi-leveled approach to the processes of finding out and investigating stories.

If we step back and examine our own adult storying lives, we discover that narrative is indeed part of all our thought. Accepting this, we can no longer dismiss storytelling and story-reading merely as effective tools in approaching "real" writing and reading. We must take seriously Harold Rosen's proposal that we look at the whole school curriculum from the point of view of its narrative possibilities: narrative must become a more acceptable way of saying, writing, thinking, and presenting. We're proposing not that anecdote should drive out analysis, but that narrative should be allowed its honorable place in the analysis of everything.

## Sharing Stories

The case for the sharing of stories is literally as old as language. The people of early societies seem to have valued their oral literature as an entertaining, memorable means of making sense of the world they saw about them, of the behaviour of their fellows, and of themselves. In Ted Hughes's terms, such tales linked inner and outer worlds. The coherence of the stories offered the hope of coherence in life itself. The North-West Coastal Indians of North America, for example, accorded a tribal storyteller the status of a chieftain; upon him depended the health of the community — his tales of ravens and salmon, bears and eagles, told how the animals had prepared the world and given it a pattern in readiness for the arrival of mankind. The storyteller's magic, like that of the Anglo-Saxon scop, the medieval minstrel or the eighteenth-century balladmonger, (or even a rabbit named Dandelion in *Watership Down*), lay in bringing dead words to life in the imaginations of his audience. The value of shared story and poetry today is of no less importance than it was for the tribal community.

Geoff Fox and Michael Benton,
*Teaching Literature from Nine to Fourteen*[7]

We like a workshop approach to story exploration. We begin with a valuable shared story experience, building on the spontaneity, the intensity, the organic strength of the initial experience of the story.

During our years of teaching, we have spent a great deal of time sharing stories, listening and reading together, as would a tribe around the campfire. There are public meanings within stories that trigger universal meanings for all of us experiencing the story, as well as private meanings for each individual involved. Even the shared meanings will have private aspects, since each of us makes our own stories in our minds based on our unique life experiences. However, these shared ideas unite us, join us together in common expectations and awareness. After we listen or read and experience, we can then story together, exploring our common experiences, clarifying our own questions, altering our public and private stories, building story frames for "us" as well as for "me". The collective, collaborative stories we make are as significant as those we have read or heard to begin with. A story is a story, and if we have ownership and authorship, the story is part of us forever. Much of school is individualized, and that is as it should be. A book, after all, is a one-on-one affair between author and reader. Yet if we are gathered together by clans in schoolrooms, can we not cooperate and collaborate on making new story meanings that can affect all of us?

As children respond to a story together, their responses engender new storying activities. We begin with the shared, common story, and we talk ourselves into accepting the elements and components that build a story for us as a tribe. We use this public story to shape and stimulate new stories using all modes of response. As a cast performs one play, we as a group read one story. There will be at the same time stories, unique and private, happening in every individual's mind, stimulated by the responding and exploring, by the collaborating and cooperating, that occur when we work as one. The storyteller tells, the listeners react, as audience and as individuals, simultaneously. We are in the tribal circle, and we are each of us members. What stories hold! Words never known, yet immediately understood. Patterns of language seldom, if ever, used by the children — literary structures that carry a heritage of thought from our linguistic past, translations from other cultures rich in sound and sense, melodies and rhythms that tune the ear to the power of words (e.g., metaphors, images, and analogies for making meaning from our story senses). Thirty-six children give us thirty-six times the language power of our "teacher" voices.

Children new to English find in a story context for understanding. It is not word lists that command their attention, but the lives of the characters that fill the tales they read or listen to, both in the stories of their classmates and in the literary stories they meet. How painful it must be for those children alien to English to sit day after day without feeling connected to what is happening in the classroom. And yet, through storying, how quickly they can enter the activity, make sense of what is happening, building their own versions, listening, telling, retelling; talking about, reflecting upon — responding.

Teacher and children must build a supportive and collaborative atmosphere where everyone sits inside the story circle and is part of the storying experience. In a shared story experience, teachers should regroup physically the class into a "theatre mode" so that the story can be presented in the strongest way possible. The children may sit around us, or we may somehow group them so there is a sense of belonging to the experience. The teacher's voice and demeanor will be part of this, and he or she has to be aware of the audience contact and of how the story is being experienced. Commercially available tapes and records to complement the teacher's own tellings and readings, readers' theatre presentations by rehearsed groups, professional storytellers, guests, student teachers, and parents — they can all be part of the community of readers who celebrate storying with children.

When we read aloud to children, we prepare them for reading on their own. We introduce them to what Frank Smith called the literacy club, and give them reasons for wanting to read. They become acquainted with the varied languages of story, with predicting and anticipating what will come next, with the patterns of story structures from all cultures. They become familiar with the rhythms and structures, the cadences and conventions of the various forms of written language. They are learning how print sounds, how to hear it in their inner ear.

Bringing the words of someone other than yourself to life is the major task facing the person who reads aloud. Interpreting someone else's words demands that we be faithful to what an author has written, but it calls for just as much use of imagination as of storytelling. Readers must project themselves into the lives and emotions of others and in doing so take some liberties in interpreting the text to create the right feeling.

For these reasons, it is essential that the text we choose to read aloud be prepared ahead of time and that some care be given to the physical relationship of book, reader, and audience.

Many stories recommended for storytelling lend themselves equally well to reading aloud. For young children, pattern that supports prediction is important. Stories rich in texture which can be read again and again are also important. For this reason, picture books make a good choice. Books such as *Grandpa* by John Burningham or *A Walk in the Park* by Anthony Browne invite continual revisiting and stimulate much talk and interest. But more important, books read aloud by the teacher become "bestsellers" overnight in the classroom. For young children growing into reading, picture books sustain, through illustration, youngsters' attempts to make meaning with the text.

Because reading aloud permits the teacher to concentrate on the rhythms and sounds of language, words that invite improvisation can be one criterion for selection. Author/illustrator William Steig has a delicious knack for word play. Almost everything he has written is a delight to read aloud. Here's a tiny snippet from *Brave Irene*:

The wind wrestled her for the package — walloped it, twisted it, shook it, snatched at it. But Irene wouldn't yield. It's my mother's work! She screamed. Then — oh woe! — the box was wrenched from her mittened grasp and sent bumbling along in the snow. Irene went after it.[8]

Interesting rhythms also characterize Steig's work; this is another feature to look for — not necessarily smooth rhythms, but uneven ones. Kevin Crossley-Holland's retellings of English folktales are filled with such examples.

The three young men walked around the draughty palace; they wondered through the shining gardens, and into the stables. And there perched on a lintel, was a beautiful bird.

She was gold and she was turquoise, and she sang their aches away.
Let's catch her, said One
And cage her, said Two[9]

Also consider stories which explore subtleties of character. Some of the all-time favorite stories of children remain so for this very reason. *John Brown, Rose and the Midnight Cat* (Jenny Wagner); *Little Bear* (Else Holmelund Minarik), *Frog and Toad* (Arnold Lobel); *The wheel on the School* (Meindert De Jong); *Sarah, Plain and Tall* (Patricia MacLachlan); *The One-Eyed Cat* (Paula Fox) all come to mind as good examples.

With young adolescents it is often thought that stories must necessarily be fast-paced and tinged with gore to capture this seemingly complacent audience. "Mr. Fox" (Grimm) may indeed be what is required from time to time, but it needn't become a steady diet. Of course, *Scary Tales to Tell in the Dark* (Alvin Schwartz) goes down well with these young people, but so too do "Silent Bianca" (Jane Yolen, in *The Girl Who Cried Flowers*) and "The Rose and the Minor Demon" in *The Devil's Storybook* (Natalie Babbitt). Adolescents may appear worldly on the outside, but deep down they want to learn about life's complexities. Stories emphasizing human relationships are important to them, but the material mustn't be preachy or didactic. Like all of us, they respond to a good yarn. Don't overlook folk and fairy tales with these youngsters. This may be exactly the time in their lives when these stories will really connect with them.

At the conclusion of storytelling or reading aloud there may be no need to introduce a follow-up activity. Letting the story settle into the landscape of individual imagination may be quite sufficient. If the children keep talking about the story or seem to need further involvement with aspects of it, then capitalize on it. Occasionally a longer story which is being presented serially over a number of days may require some extra attention, especially if there are gaps of a day or more between sessions or if the story is slow to hook the listeners.

Whether you tell a story or read it aloud may depend upon the tale, *the story itself* (How literary is it? Should the author's voice be retained?); the told, *the children* (Do they need the immediacy of the storyteller? Should they see an adult reading from a text?); and the teller, *you the teacher* (Do you need the support of the print? Are you familiar with the story? Will the children want to join in?). Some stories we know so well that we read them as if we were telling them from our hearts.

The stories we choose to read are those that we enjoy ourselves. Every time we share one with a group of children, we find new meanings to interpret aloud. It may be a word with a delicious sound, a dialogue in which we can employ different voices, a mood that can be created with careful modulation, a feeling conjured up by the artful magic of the writer. As you become familiar with a story, you will find yourself maintaining eye contact with the children, sensing their responses so that you can build upon them. If you are using a picture book, then the illustrations are telling the story as well. How important that the children have an opportunity to notice the father and the children in Anthony Browne's *Piggybook* turning literally into pigs, or the similarity of the father and the gorilla in Browne's *Gorilla*. Sometimes, the pictures can be saved for a second telling, so that the story is uninterrupted the first time. Children will use the illustrations later for their own storytelling of both literary and personal anecdotes.

Reading a special novel aloud over a period of time can develop anticipation and speculation if the children are enjoying the experience. Choose a novel of depth, one that they might not choose, and build on it upon completion as a unit or theme of study. *The Machine-Gunners* by Robert Westall, set in wartime Britain fifty years ago, is both challenging and breathtaking when read aloud well.

Storytelling may be the oldest of all the arts. The mother told the story to her child, the hunter to his peers, the survivor to his rescuers, the priestess to her followers, the seer to his petitioners. The better the tale was told, the more it was believed and remembered. When we read or tell a story aloud, we release it from the printed page, we give it life.

We can't all tell the same stories. There are some we are drawn to immediately and others which just don't seem to succeed. British educator Dorothy Heathcote says that the skills of teaching lie in making time slow enough for inquiry, interesting enough to loiter along the way, and rigorous enough to bring new thought processes into understanding.[10] Stories are invaluable to the teacher because they permit the child time to daydream; they let the mind wander; they sharpen perception and the reflective processes.

Bill Martin, Jr. says that stories spoken aloud "set the sounds of language ringing in our ears," thus preserving the stories' strengths and causing them to remain with us long after the telling.[11] Good words hold the mind and enhance comprehension because of their rich appeal to the imagination. A love of sound is indispensable to the love of words and, hence, to their understanding. Folktales, sifted as they have been, through hundreds of years of telling, carry only the words necessary for compelling and imaginative communication.

It is not necessary to change the words to suit the age level of the audience. The imagination of the child and the context of the story usually supply the keys to understanding. Many of the more difficult words contribute atmosphere by their mere sound; it doesn't always matter what they mean. As author Joan Aiken says, "Things not understood have a radiance of their own."[12]

Stories will develop in children an understanding of structure so they can predict what new stories they would like. They will come to expect a consistent structure — a definite beginning, middle, and ending; they will come to expect the resolution of a problem which will leave them feeling satisfied; they will develop a set of characters and situations, thus providing them with a kind of story shorthand for dealing with complex notions such as wickedness or deceit.

There are always reactions from listeners that reveal something about the story that the storyteller may not have noticed or known. By watching the listeners, a teacher can come to a new understanding, and he or she and the class can have a new and enriching experience. The pleasure that arises between speaker and listener rests on the teller's interpretation, which may — or may not — stimulate the listener's imagination to set the scene, visualize the players, and follow the action. The voice, expression, gestures, and imagination of the storyteller are powerful factors in determining whether the audience experiences a story vividly and creatively.

If the teacher is enthusiastic about a story and sincerely motivated to tell it, genuine success with storying will likely follow.

It is important that enjoyment be conveyed in the stories the teacher reads and tells.

It is also important that the teacher constantly adapt the program to fit the needs of the group. Charles Reasoner asks the questions: Do you display the book in advance so children can browse through it to see if they wish to make plans to attend? When it is story time, do you give children time to finish their work, a five- or ten-minute warning? Do you have them in a comfortable position? If they are sitting on the floor, is it warm enough? Is the lighting adequate? Are you standing or sitting so they have to hold their heads uncomfortably? Can the children at the back of the room see you and, if there are any, the pictures? Can you read the story a second time if the class so chooses? Do you draw attention away from the story with unnatural gestures or a voice that is loud, strained, or phony? Do you talk down to young audiences? Do you patronize them? Do you tag a moral ending onto a story so that it's unnecessarily anticlimactic? Do you interrupt the story, do you break the mood, the magic, the flow for a teaching commercial or a vocabulary lesson? If a child has disturbed the story-reading, do you seat him within arm's reach? Do you put off questions or anecdotes volunteered by children by shaking your head slightly or changing expression? Do you time the story so that it comes at a convenient time for children's energies, for the rhythm of the class? Do you read stories to the children they would not normally read for themselves? Do you interpret each story to its fullest? Do you relate and connect stories from one period to another so that a story repertoire emerges? Do you give children time to respond to a story?[13]

There are many ways to help children involve themselves in experiencing a story. Through active participation by retelling or re-creating the story, through chanting and experimenting with rhythms and moods, through improvisation, the teacher can create opportunities for giving context and meaning. (If, for instance, a child assumes a role in a story and enacts particular situations, he or she begins to find personal meaning in it.)

Telling a story is not a difficult task to master, especially if a simple repetitive or cumulative tale is chosen. There is a story by Linda Williams called *The Little Old Lady Who Wasn't Afraid of Anything* which makes a good example.

The plot is simple. A little old lady goes into the woods to collect nuts and berries and seeds. She stays too late and is overtaken by night. As she rushes along the path home she encounters a pair of clomping boots, wriggling trousers, a flapping shirt, two white gloves, a tall black hat, and eventually a large, scary jack-o'-lantern. All chase the old woman to her house, where she barricades herself behind locked doors. But she is the little old lady who isn't afraid of anything, isn't she? How she handles her dilemma is both clever and funny.

Because the story is repetitive and cumulative and supports prediction, the telling of it invites much chiming in. For example, each meeting (e.g., "Right in the middle of the path were two big shoes") is followed by a description of the noise the object makes ("and the shoes went CLOMP, CLOMP").

Each time the old woman flees from an object the words, "But behind her she could hear..." are repeated.[14]

Ever so slight a pause each time the teller approaches these bits of the story never fails to elicit the vocal prediction of the listeners.

As the children get caught up in the mystery and fun, chiming in with known bits, their confidence grows and the story, borne on the playful and imaginative interchange between teller and audience, comes to life magnificently.

If you want to try storytelling, you'll need to pay some attention to selecting, shaping, and presenting a story, but the main thing is to plunge in. There are hundreds of thousands of stories to choose from and, as indicated earlier, folktales make excellent source material. Not only are these stories closest to the natural storying of children, but also they possess such qualities as immediacy, surprise, and the provision of support for the children's predictions about story that make them ideal. They also often offer the teller opportunities for outstanding oral performance. In *The World of Storytelling*, Anne Pellowski discusses the different styles that storytellers in various cultures use to begin and end stories, particular phrases and expressions that demonstrate customs in other locales.[15]

A question frequently asked of storytellers is, "Do you tell the story the way it is in the book?" There are probably as many answers to that question as there are storytellers, for how a story is brought to life is central to storytelling. Certainly it is essential that the storyteller remain faithful to the core of the story, but how each person embellishes the story is what makes storytelling such an exciting art-form. Here's one way to approach story.

After reading the story once, slowly, make an outline of it in your own words and then try telling it to yourself. A second reading of the story will reveal if any significant details have been omitted.

Read the story a third time and consider the feelings and attitudes of the story characters. Try telling it to yourself again.

On the fourth reading pay close attention to the language of the story. What words or phrases should be preserved to retain the story's unique sound? Tell the story again to yourself.

A fifth reading might be devoted to blocking the story into scenes and considering the sensory details (lights, sounds, colors, etc.). Now tell the story to yourself again.

A final reading should concentrate on the beginning and ending. A strong start and a confident finish are important: you may want to memorize the beginning and ending of the story.

There are various editing techniques that might also be employed (e.g., condensing the story; elaborating on something only hinted at; dropping an extraneous character; converting dialogue to narrative or vice versa; rearranging the plot, especially if the story's exposition is particularly long; experimenting with the narrative style). Insight into the kind of shaping a story requires becomes more apparent after you have told yourself the story a few times.

The real test of your telling comes when you face your audience. Storytelling is an audience-valuing situation. The storyteller should feel the audience response throughout and continually modify the delivery accordingly. The important thing is to start slowly, watch carefully the responses of your listeners, and maintain your concentration. See your story, feel it — make everything happen. Use the voice you use in everyday conversation and respond naturally to your feelings about the story. As for gestures and body language, let them be natural as well. With practice you will quickly learn what is right for your own style and delivery.

Some teachers gain more confidence telling a story when they actively involve the children in some way:

Stories with repetitive choruses or motifs provide the easiest means of involvement.

Usually, when listening to stories containing repetitions and refrains, children will join in automatically. Once they are familiar with the repeated parts, a slight pause by the teller is all that is necessary to invite their response. Wanda Gag's "hundreds of cats, thousands of cats" refrain is a famous example. Nursery rhymes such as this one are good sources too.

> If all the seas were one sea
> what a great sea that would be.
>
> If all the trees were one tree
> What a great tree that would be.
>
> If all beings were one being
> What a great being that would be.
>
> If all the axes were one axe
> What a great axe that would be.
>
> And if the great being took the great axe
> and chopped down the great tree,
>
> And if the great tree fell into the great sea
> What a great SPLASH that would be.

## CALL AND RESPONSE

Stories or songs with a question-and-answer format are among the most common sources for call-and-response storytelling. Most people are familiar with this example: "'There's a hole in the bucket, dear Liza, dear Liza. There's a hole in the bucket, dear Liza, a hole!'

"Well fix it, dear Henry, dear Henry, dear Henry. Well fix it, dear Henry, dear Henry, fix it."

Some of the best call-and-response stories can be found in folksongs and games, narrative poetry, nursery rhymes, ballads, and song sermons.

## TRACING RITUAL PATTERN

Stories told by the community in song and dance live on in some of the practices observed by children as they participate in playground rituals associated with turning skipping ropes, choosing sides for games, and clapping out rhythmical chants. These singing/dancing stories are still found in a variety of sources including records and tapes. Other sources to explore include books on active games, nursery rhyme collections, and Iona and Peter Opie's *Children's Games in Street and Playground*, as well as their magnificent *The Singing Games*.[16]

The following example was adapted from *Children's Games in Street and Playground*. It is sung to the tune of ''Hang Down Your Head, Tom Dooley'' and restructured as a play using movement with almost no spoken words.

There are a king, a queen, a princess, a captain of the quard, and some soldiers, as well as a castle, which consists of two children holding hands. The king tells the captain of the guard to march round the castle singing:

> Will you surrender, will you surrender,
> To the King of the Barbarees?

The Castle:
> We won't surrender, we won't surrender,
> To the King of the Barbarees.

Captain:
> I'll tell the King, I'll tell the King,
> The King of the Barbarees.

The Castle:
> You can tell the King, you can tell the King,
> The King of the Barbarees.

The captain goes back to the king and, stamping his feet, says,

> They won't surrender, they won't surrender,
> The King of the Barbarees.

The king says, ''Take two of my trusty soldiers.''
The soldiers follow the captain and the rhyme is repeated again:

> Will you surrender, will you surrender,
> To the King of the Barbarees?

This goes on until all the soldiers have joined the ring, then the king says, "Take my daughter." Next to go is the queen, and last of all the king. The king says, "We'll break down your gates," and after the rhyme has been said again with the king joining in, everybody holds hands to form a line between the castle and the king. He takes a run and tries to break through the line, while the two who are the castle count to ten. If he does not break through, he goes back and one of the soldiers has a turn. They all take a run at the line, one at a time, and try to break it down. If they do not succeed the castle has won.

As children become comfortable gaming with word and structure and rhythm and movement, larger narrative sequences can become the source for out-loud exploration. Narrative poetry and traditional folktales treated in simple story theatre techniques might be attempted next (see Chapter 3).

## A Model for Storying

We have seen many "story" classrooms in our travels. One excellent model is that described in the following journal piece by Alan Newland, a teacher in England.

I'm beginning to realise the power of story telling. It's a beginning for me, because outside of reading books aloud to my class, I had never really stopped to think about how often we all tell stories; out loud, in our heads, everywhere and all the time, these stories are simple anecdotes which are left undeveloped. Working from an idea by a colleague, we began to explore ways in which the seemingly insignificant trivia of everyday lives could be made more meaningful.

'The Patchwork Quilt' by Valerie Flournoy is a book about connecting the scraps of one's shared existence into a significant whole. A little girl, housebound by a cold, watches her granny put together a quilt from the scraps of her family's old clothing. But the granny falls seriously ill, and the task of finishing the quilt is taken up at first by the little girl and then by her mother. The quilt's completion becomes an act of faith in their grandmother's recovery, and her recovery in turn a powerful assertion of women arts and crafts, of the 'old' values that the granny was so frightened had been lost by her daughter's generation, and of the significance of their shared experience as a family.

I asked the children in my class of third year junior to bring in treasured possessions from their earliest memories; old clothes, favourite toys, family photographs. We sat in a circle and talked about them. We giggled at each other's teddy bears, sailing boats, old snap-shots and listened to the stories behind them. One story led to another, and although they were all different, like the quilt in the story, we began connecting our patches with a common thread.

Once a week we spent the whole morning doing this and the children not only became engrossed in each other's life stories, but they listened, reflected and told new ones with a rapidly developing competence.

I wondered where this competence came from. It was learned, that was obvious because I could see them learning it; but it wasn't taught, at least not by me. Were they teaching it to each other and if so, how?

Their concern for each other was obvious. Interruptions were few and confined to making connections of common interests. We would alternate between talking in twos and threes and gathering together to share as a class. As the first few weeks passed with the children bringing in more and more photos, old toys, watches, musical instruments, heirlooms and treasured possessions of every kind, it became apparent that a peculiar kind of sharing was going on.

One week a girl brought in a piece of dress material worn by her mother as a maternity smock, accompanied by a letter written by mum recalling the days spent wearing it. A broken old watch was given to one child's mother as a final parting gift of a dying grandfather. The powerful and important memories evoked by attachment to such treasured objects is not difficult to comprehend, but what was more elusive to my understanding and what seemed more interesting was the re-assessing and re-shaping of experience that seemed to be going on. Changes in the way they were comprehending experience seemed to be taking place and then an incident of particular significance took place which helped me sort all this out a bit more clearly.

Two years ago my mother died and I began wearing her wedding ring. This was noticed by my class at the time and so I explained it to them. In one of our morning 'telling-story' sessions a child related an incident of finding some valuable jewellary and taking it, with her mother, to the police.

"I wouldn't do that," said Nicola, only half jokingly.

"Would you?" I asked.

"Yeh!" she replied, "finders keepers, innit? Or sell it, you could take it down the jewellery shop and sell it."

Some others agreed, especialy if you could sell it. Then someone reminded us all that "you wouldn't like it if it was your jewellery that was lost though, would you?"

Here I saw my chance to intervene. I took off my mother's ring and held it out to Nicola. Her eyes were fixed on it and she was understandably apprehensive. She knew what I was going to ask.

"What would you do if you found this one Nic? Would you sell it?"

She didn't answer, but smiled back at me nervously.

"Go on, hold it," I said trying to reassure her, but her friend Tanya, sitting next to her, came to her aid.

"No you can't sell that," she said quietly, "it's part of your mum."

Everyone was quiet, though not embarrassed.

"But how do we know that that lost jewellery wasn't just as important to the person who lost it as this ring is to me?" I asked. At that moment, I could almost see the stories swirling about their heads as to why that jewellery might be important to someone. So I asked them; "Why do you think that jewellery was important to the person who lost it?" Some of the stories that followed were short and simple, others were elaborate and beautiful. "Everything's important to someone, sometime, isn't it?" said Natalie, a nine year old. I sat looking at her, thinking what an incredible insight that was for a mind so young, but it was also an observation which, on reflection, seemed to show an enormous grasp of the limitless possibilities of narrative.

So when stories are told by children, our role (apart from listening to them) is to imbue them with meaning. They are not simply anecdotes but appraisals of their experiences. Their confidence grows, and out of it gradually blossoms a cognition that what they say appears to have significance for others; "oh yeh, that reminds me of the time when ..." or "that's just like when I was going to ..." The full blooming of this cognizance comes when children begin to focus on the most fleeting of memories or the minutest of details and expand them into self contained stories with an integral structure.

They become more confident because their experience is being validated, what was significant is becoming significant to themselves and to others ...

Oral narrative is not just a powerful way of validating one's life to oneself and to others but it can also be a useful tool of analysis and for assimilating one's understanding of scientific and technical concepts. How do we grasp such things as the big bang theory, evolution or the behaviour of the aids virus when it attacks cells, or anything we don't have the technical expertise to understand? Indeed, who has ever had, save perhaps Einstein, the technical capacity to comprehend such things? Quite simply, we describe it to ourselves as a story. Jerome Bruner has discussed at length the role of narrative and its relationship to the development of scientific concepts and Harold Rosen also argues very powerfully that narrative should be raised to 'its honourable place in the analysis of everything' ...

My experience in recent months leads me to believe strongly that allowing children the time to tell each other their stories, finding ways of making connections, validating each other's experiences and sharing meanings, is giving children a sense of significance and a self-knowledge which could have powerful repercussions beyond the classroom and into their homes and communities.[17]

## The Teacher's Voice

The decisive matter is how the teacher's imagination

engages with the text — a prelude, naturally, to the students' engagement.

Robert Coles,<br>
*The Call of Stories*[18]

Does the classroom teacher's own use of story and of language affect the students? How important are our own skills in speaking and listening, reading and writing? What types of language behavior do we exhibit with our students during our time with them? Do the students learn from us an unwritten curriculum in languaging by simply observing, interacting with, and listening to us? Of course, our use of language can have a powerful effect on the children. The teacher must read aloud, if not with the skills of a trained voice, at least with an understanding of what is being read and with a determination to read it with integrity and commitment. We need to put words and spoken language to efficient use, selecting carefully, powerfully, and economically the words that best fit the purpose we put them to.

Because story is a particular way of learning, the teacher must be very sensitive to language when telling a story, so that as much as possible can be revealed at any moment. As well, it is important to develop a good ear for language effect, a wide range of tone, effective volume and pitch. This sounds challenging, but take heart! The children will lead us to the language well. By working alongside the children, by trying on different roles and voices in the safety of the story experience, and by becoming passionately involved in the actions and reactions of the children, any teacher will learn with the children.

If it is true that the most valuable language learning happens when students are intellectually and emotionally involved, then shouldn't it be true for the teacher as well? While the story for the teacher and the story for children may be different, the language needs of both remain constant: to communicate appropriately and effectively and to understand enough to become involved in the making of meaning, both private and public. The teacher, freed from the traditional patterns of classroom interaction, will be able to use different patterns of language in storytelling. His or her language should be accessible, encouraging, and exploratory.

The teacher's personal languaging abilities are important after the storytelling as well. The teacher should be able to rework the class talk about the story where necessary — elevating, elaborating, extending, focusing, altering the mood or the tone; and always, in a supportive manner, encouraging the participation of the children and honing the quality of their language and thought. The art of language is the heart of teaching. Story is one medium that deeply values the language of both teacher and student. It provides an opportunity for us as teachers to learn along with the children, and lets us share in their exploration of language.

FORGOTTEN LANGUAGE

Once I spoke the language of the flowers,
Once I understood each word the caterpillar
    said,
Once I smiled in secret at the gossip of the
    starlings,
And shared a conversation with the housefly in
    my bed.
Once I heard and answered all the questions of
    the crickets,
And joined the crying of each falling dying flake
    of snow,
Once I spoke the language of the flowers . . .
How did it go?
How did it go?

Shel Silverstein[19]

Wayne Booth says that who we are is best shown by the stories we can tell and who we can become is best determined by the stories we can learn to tell.[20] As teachers, we can make what we want of any story with our children; but what stories will we choose to tell? We as teachers want to belong to the tribe, to contribute our tales, to listen to those of other members, and to share in the stories we create together. The classroom is a village of stories and storymakers. We as well as the children belong to it; we too have stories to tell.

CHAPTER **3**

# *A Story Inventory*

AUNT SUE'S STORIES

Aunt Sue has a head full of stories.
Aunt Sue has a whole heart full of stories.
Summer nights on the front porch
Aunt Sue cuddles a brown-faced child to her
  bosom
And tells him stories.

Black slaves
Working in the hot sun,
And black slaves
Walking in the dewy night,
And black slaves
Singing sorrow songs on the banks of the
  mighty river
Mingle themselves softly
In the flow of old Aunt Sue's voice,
Mingle themselves softly
In the dark shadows that cross and recross
Aunt Sue's stories.

And the dark-faced child, listening,
Knows that Aunt Sue's stories are real stories.
He knows that Aunt Sue
Never got her stories out of any book at all,
But that they came
Right out of her own life.

And the dark-faced child is quiet
Of a summer night
Listening to Aunt Sue's stories.

Langston Hughes[1]

## How the Story Chooses Us

> The story itself is an acquisition, a kind of wealth. We only
> have to imagine for a moment an individual who knows noth-
> ing of it at all. His ignorance would shock us, and, in a real
> way, he would be outside our society. How would he even
> begin to understand most of the ideas which are at the roots
> of our culture and appear everywhere among the branches?
>
> Ted Hughes[2]

This chapter focuses on the written story, narratives transcribed
or authored for others to read or listen to. Some of the stories
have grown from oral tales, from talk anecdotes artfully arranged
on paper, but we will be discussing the story in print as a means
of increasing the literary storehouse of each child and of developing in all children a belief in and a sense of story. Where do we
find all these stories, and which ones will appeal to the children?

Story selection is highly personal. The stories we grow to love
are not necessarily perfect examples of the art, nor are they
always the ones we started out to find. The element of surprise
is very much alive where story selection is concerned.

The different ways in which each of us has come to stories
will figure prominently in what we take into our classrooms to
share. These personal encounters with stories are important —
indeed, often the story has found us, not vice versa.

> I found the book on a second-hand bookstall shortly after
> the war and the moment I read: "I am a virgin twelve years
> of age," my attention was riveted and the last page came
> for me too soon.
>
> Honor Arundel on "The Book of Maggie Owen"
> in *Author's Choice*[3]

Author and teacher Bill Martin, Jr. describes his story journey:

> My first book reading came when I was twenty. In college.
> Yes, then even nonreaders were admitted to college or
> university if they could muster tuition fees. By this time in
> my life I was so skilled in masking my print blindness that
> most teachers thought I was lazy, unprepared, never

suspecting that it was my ears, not my eyes, that opened Sesame. I have Miss Davis to thank. She tuned my ears to literate language, to the voice of the text. Not to the voice of Jack London, but to the voice of his story, "To Build a Fire." Not to the voice of Robert Louis Stevenson, but to the voice of *Treasure Island*. Not to the voice of James Whitcomb Riley, but to the voice of "Little Orphan Annie." Not to the voice of Daniel DeFoe, but to the voice of *Robinson Crusoe*. Now, years later, I have learned to search the page for the voice of the text in determining whether to devote reading time to an unfamiliar book. In this context, *voice* and *comprehension* are synonymous.[4]

It seems obvious that exposure to a lot of stories early on is an important part of our learning about them, but so too is an attitude of openness like that of Honor Arundel. That attitude of openness to stories has never been better described than in the words of this Maori storyteller:

> The breath of life,
> The spirit of life,
> The word of life,
> It flies to you and you and you
> Always the word.[5]

And we return to one of the resonances of this book — pay attention to the story, regard the images that fill your mind, trust the story to do its work. And what is a story?

> Something with a beginning, a middle, and an end, of course. But the lasting stories are more. If they are lacking that bit of "inner truth," if they do not make Dinesen's "serious statement," then they are of no value. Without meaning, without metaphor, without reaching out to touch human emotion, a story is a poor thing: a few rags upon a stick masquerading as a living creature.
> Jane Yolen, *Favorite Folktales from around the World*[6]

Once we have discovered a story or the story has discovered

us, it grows in our imaginations. Over time, comparisons are made with like tales; variants, especially if we are dealing with stories from the oral tradition, are found; familiar motifs are recognized; and story history and relatives come to be understood. Stories connecting stories, patterns, pathways, relationships criss and cross like skeins of wool on a loom and we are drawn into the pattern, fascinated, filled with the anticipation of new discoveries.

OWL TROUBLE

Crows detest you.
With his sharp eyes, one spots you,
lets out a 'caw'
that tells the others
you are here.
Gathering around you
perching as close as possible
cawing at the top of their black voices,
tormenting until you can stand it no longer.
You fly off
with a scream
followed by this noisy black mob,
this tail of tormentors.
Owl, you frighten me.
Owl, you fascinate me.

David Booth[7]

A momentary observation, "Crows detest you"; an act of panic, "You fly off with a scream"; a statement of emotion, "Owl, you fascinate me." Resonances of stories from all over the world cry out their "owl lore."

WHY HENS ARE AFRAID OF OWLS

Once upon a time, hens had dances every Saturday night. They employed Mr. Owl for a fiddler. He was always careful to go away before daylight so that the hens might not see his big eyes. The last time he fiddled for them, daylight caught him, and when the hens had a look at his eyes they were frightened into fits and went squalling out of the room.

Ever since then, the hen cannot even bear the shadow of an owl.

Roger Abrahams,
*Afro American Folktales*[8]

Owl hiding his eyes. How like the story of Owl in the wonderful collection of Haitian folktales, *The Magic Orange Tree*, by Diane Wolkstein, where "Owl thought he was ugly" so he moved freely only in shadow and darkness until he fell in love.

Shadow and darkness. The fate of Owl in "The Hedge King", retold by the Brothers Grimm, where Owl incurs the wrath of all the birds when he fails to keep as prisoner the tiny "hedge bird" who has just cheated in the contest to name a king of the birds. As punishment, Owl is banished to the night world and badgered by all birds if he shows his face by day.

Shows his face by day. Certainly something Owl in Ted Hughes's story *How the Owl Became* can never do again. Here is played out a macabre tale in which Owl, a master of cunning and deceit, almost succeeds in enslaving the entire feather-and-claw population. The incredible exodus led by Owl, through rabbit warrens underground, makes for compelling reading and telling.

*The Man Who Could Call Down Owls* is a powerful tale of revenge, as Charles Mikolaycak's black and white illustrations paint a world of feathers and night. When the owls attack the imposter who has murdered the one who could call them down, the story gruesomely demonstrates the strange and precarious balance of nature.

Why are there owls in these stories? Are they themes and metaphors, allegories, ideas, or birds (or all of the above)?

## Story Sets

As teachers, we can help the children classify or categorize stories by genre, type, theme, or story attributes. Consider the options:

| | |
|---|---|
| Variations of the same folktale | *Dawn* by Molly Bang. *The Crane Wife* by Katherine Paterson. Adaptations of a Japanese legend. |

| | |
|---|---|
| Cultural variants of the same tale | "The Invisible Boy" in Alden Nowlan's *Nine Micmac Legends*. An Indian Cinderella story. |
| Different versions of the same story | "Tom Poker" in Allan Garner's *A Bag of Moonshine*. Who is stronger — Sun, Wind, or Cloud? |
| Same story pictured by different illustrators | *The Wild Swans* by Hans Christian Andersen. Illustrated by Angela Barrett. *The Wild Swans*. Illustrated by Helen Stratton. |
| Stories with similar structures | *The Cat Who Loved to Sing* by Nonny Hogrogian. *Hattie and the Fox* by Mem Fox. Cumulative structures. |
| Stories on a particular theme or topic | *Ananci Spiderman* by James Berry. Stories of the West Indian trickster/hero. |
| Tales of specific genres — ballads, etc. | *Proud Knight, Fair Lady* by Naomi Lewis (trans.). The Twelve Lays of Marie de France. |
| Books by one author or illustrator | *Collected Stories* by Richard Kennedy. Illustrated by Marcia Sewall. |
| Stories with the same characters | *Tales of the Early World* by Ted Hughes. God is portrayed as an artist creating the earth's creatures. |
| Stories from the same culture. | *Three Indian Princesses* by Jamila Gavin. Three heroines from the folktales of India. |
| Stories with similar motifs | *The Buffalo Boy and the Weaver Girl* by Mary Alice Downie. *The Selchie Girl* by Susan Cooper. *The Buffalo Woman* by Paul Goble. Taboo: giving garment back to supernatural wife. |

The following chart examines one motif in story — animals — and then explores the many classifications that can emerge. Children can read and listen to selections from one category, or groups can compare stories for attributes in order to classify them.

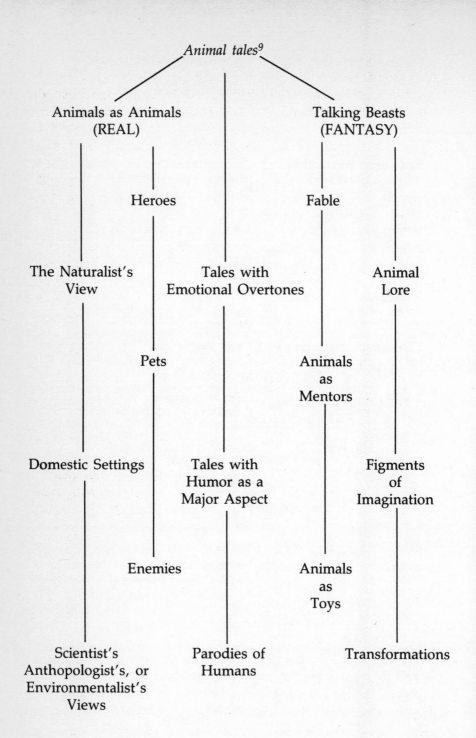

*Animal tales*[9]

Animals as Animals
(REAL)

Talking Beasts
(FANTASY)

Heroes

Fable

The Naturalist's
View

Tales with
Emotional Overtones

Animal
Lore

Pets

Animals
as
Mentors

Domestic Settings

Tales with
Humor as a
Major Aspect

Figments
of
Imagination

Enemies

Animals
as
Toys

Scientist's
Anthopologist's, or
Environmentalist's
Views

Parodies of
Humans

Transformations

As we journey along story pathways we may suddenly find a story we passed just recently reappearing with new life, new vitality (stories connecting stories, and stories being recreated). Kevin Crossley-Holland's recent reworking of fifty-five or so British folktales is but one thread in a history of storytelling that goes back to Homer and includes such famous personages as Aesop, Mme. de Beaumont, Hans Christian Andersen, Oscar Wilde, Laurence Houseman, and Isaac Bashevis Singer. Sometimes retellings become so popular that a story's original roots are forgotten. Perrault's reworking of "Cinderella", for example, eventually outshone its five hundred or so variants and remains to this day one of the most popular fairy tales in the world.

Our personal journeys through story and stories, our memories of stories which have reached out and touched us, must be our guide in helping us to find the stories we want to share in our classrooms. Combined with this must be our knowledge of the children we work with and our hunches about what will speak to them. There are parameters to guide us: diversity is one of these. A wide variety of material is essential.

Thousands of children's titles pour from the presses of Great Britain, Canada, Australia, New Zealand, and the United States each year. Obviously, keeping up with this output is impossible for a classroom teacher, yet the teacher who wants to bring to children an appreciation of stories must be prepared to read, read, read. Of course, there are published lists of recommended titles and reviews in journals and periodicals. These are all available to guide the teacher, but there is no substitute for reading as widely as possible from the vast amount of children's literature which is available.

Among the questions teachers most often ask about children's books are:

- What sure-fire hits can you show us?
- What follow-up ideas can you give us?

The first question is tricky because in order to find "sure-fire" hits you must read a lot of books, talk to a lot of readers, and take some risks. Not everyone likes the same thing.

When it comes to follow-up ideas there is little doubt that what we do must help readers to be aware of what has taken place inside their heads as they read and to pay attention to the responses which other individuals in the class have formulated.

When making decisions about the kinds of stories that should be available in the classroom, consideration should be given not only to what the children are reading now, but also to the stories with which they are already familiar (old favorites will be reread again and again, and this is important, especially for those who are slow in reading) as well as the stories they are growing into. As one teacher put it, "At present my kids are crazy about 'Choose Your Own Adventure' books. They don't know Beverly Cleary's books or Marilyn Sachs or Philippa Pearce. I'm waiting for the right moment."

Helping children to find the right books for themselves is important, but so is the kind of flexible scheduling in school that permits children the time to get lost in a book. For many children school may be the only place where this kind of experience with a story is possible. If we are really serious about developing an early love of reading, time to read in school is fundamental.

Of course, the classroom must contain stories that enrich and extend all curriculum areas, feature picture books for all ages, offer stories that appeal to and challenge the imagination, have available books in multiple copies for small group work, and provide books representing a range of themes, genres, cultures, and authors.

Enough cannot be said about the importance of reading aloud or telling stories to your class. There is no better way for children to learn that their role as listeners is to participate in the creation of an imagined world. In having to construct an interpretation on the basis of words alone, they come to grips with the power of language to represent symbolically. As children absorb more and more stories they chime in readily and predict with increasing accuracy what is going to happen next. They relish old favorites, welcome new stories, and develop positive attitudes towards print even when the skills of reading pose a problem for them.

This means that listening to what children consider important about stories and acknowledging what they care about in stories are absolutely essential.

Surely all that matters is that children should discover for themselves the enjoyment of reading. As reading is a uniquely private and personal pleasure, this can only be a personal discovery. The role of the adult whether teacher, librarian or parent is a dual one of exposure and sensitive guidance.

Janet Hill,
*Puffin Projects and Primary Schools*[10]

In *Booktalk*, Aidan Chambers states that the art of reading lies in talking about what you have read.[11] Like all readers, children want to discuss what they have enjoyed about a story, they want to explore those aspects of the story implicit in the text and ponder the connections they have made between the story and their own lives and the lives lived in other stories.

The great challenge for teachers lies in creating environments where genuine sharing about stories can occur. Too many children associate reading with workbook tasks. Unless they are given opportunities to say in their own way what they think and feel, stories in print will mean very little to them.

Stories become memorable if children are encouraged to pose their own questions about them and to search for answers as members of a community of storytellers that includes the teacher. Although many people learn to read more or less efficiently, they don't all become readers. Important things take time, and children don't simply become book lovers overnight. They need time to build a frame of reference for stories and to become confident as readers.

Ultimately, the stories that endure with children do so because they raise questions in a way that corresponds to a child's understanding. They support the child's interest in those questions and help it grow. This brings us back to the need for an environment in which language is used creatively to examine ideas, relate occurrences, and describe shades of meaning.

Dorothy Heathcote states that it is the job of the teacher to help learners reveal what they know and give them the opportunity to care about learning more.[12] When it comes to working with children, this advice is invaluable. Central to her own work with young people has been the idea of "lengthening the period of incubation." If we look at much current practice with respect to children and stories, some clues for lengthening the

63

period of incubation may be found. For many children, a single reading of a story is followed by the answering of questions (often written) which tend to stress surface responses. Few attempts are made to draw on the children's existing oral and literate backgrounds. What might happen if we were to provide for several readings of the story, develop multi-sensory activities to enhance interpretive work, and make children aware of themselves as makers and co-makers of story?

We like to encourage children to develop a sense of ownership about their reading; to become involved in words and worlds; to respond to a story in a variety of ways; to engage in a highly social and interactive way with story. In so doing, their ability to handle a variety of texts will evolve through talk and sharing and elaborated responses.

Because we are, as teachers, part of the story community, we need to enjoy the story experience, both the text and the responses of the children. For their part, the children must have their own interests and needs met. And yet, part of our responsibility lies in sharing stories that take children far from their own worlds, stories that open up new vistas for thought and feeling, and stories that reflect their own lives and offer insights and reflection. We are building their story repertoires, and we must choose widely.

We choose stories to share that will provide an experience in storying rich enough, varied enough, that all our children will find something that they can and want to share with others.

Our stories do not always have happy endings, but they do offer hope and a future, even in coming to understand difficult situations such as loss or death. Cynicism and despair are not building blocks for children; story must leave a light shining somewhere in their eyes.

We may begin by introducing our story with a related tale or poem, or an activity that invites the children into the narrative, an anecdote from our own lives that touches on some event within the story to come, a role whereby we can set the mood or atmosphere, or draw on the experiences of the children who have prepared an introduction. One story read or told aloud can initiate the children into the next one, as stories build on one another. We like to have the stories we share available to the children for independent reading, along with related stories and media.

## Where the Stories Dwell

Picture books, folktales, poetry anthologies, and novels can give children and adolescents contexts for making meanings — personal, shared, private, and public explorations in understanding their own worlds and the worlds around them.

There are stories and stories, stories written on the sidewalks, grandmother tales, grandfather tales, endless stories, circle stories, Jack tales, tall tales — a circle of stories, with us in the middle.

Information books let children enter the world of facts, and their growing minds are eager for books that describe, explain, label, interpret, and define. Until recently, good information books at appropriate reading levels were scarce. Children could appreciate the photographs, pictures, and diagrams in a given book, but adults were needed to interpret the writing. Today, authors for children are realizing that there is a growing audience for information presented aesthetically and effectively in books geared to children's abilities and interests, as in *Shaka, King of the Zulus*, by Diane Stanley and Peter Vennema. Adults must be wary of books that purport to present facts but that have no appeal or artistic merit, no story. Everything a child reads contributes to his or her picture of what a book can offer, and information books must be no exception. Beverly Korbrin, in *Eyeopeners*, chronicles the powerful story of non-fiction, and relates it to literature.[13]

One story, one response to a story can set off an explosion of other stories — stories standing on the shoulders of others, stories within stories, stories that begin others.

Versions are wonderful things. We change stories all the time, adapting words and structures to fit the needs of every group of children. In any case, each listener is creating a unique version of the story as he or she listens. When children retell the simplest tale, so many variables appear in each version as the lives of the storytellers become enmeshed in the personal world of story. A child's background should emerge in a story he or she is sharing; if it doesn't, then what impact has the story made in that child's life? The child's identity, culture, origins will be revealed in each story told, and the resulting experience will give the original tale a pattern and texture which will enrich both the teller and the told. Rather than correct additions or alternative details, we should revel in the identification and personalizing that the child has made. Each retelling may incorporate a new dialect, different syntax, unique rhythms, particular observations, emotional shadings, specific locales, alternative time frames. The story fabric becomes elaborately embroidered as each child weaves a personal retelling.

It can be an exciting adventure for children to meet literary versions of a story they think they know. Suddenly, their preconceptions are jolted, and they move into an altered state, caught in a web of changing perception, noticing every minute difference. The story brain is engaged.

When children experience two or more stories that are related in some way, their understanding of each is altered and enriched by the other as they make connections between their expanding lives and the stories. Often one story prepares the reader for another one, facilitating the understanding of the subsequent story. And of course, each new story sheds light on past story experiences, creating a changing view of the stories in the child's story repertoire.

Children can meet all kinds of different stories and then focus on similarities and differences; individuals can each read a different story, and then share their understandings and findings.

There are many ways to organize the sharing of different but related stories — comparison charts, which demonstrate particular characteristics within different categories, samples of specific language peculiarities, emotional responses, analyses of artistic interpretations, variations in story structures, settings, cultures, or resolution. There are always different findings and insights to be shared. Fay Blostein has developed unusual and provocative themes for story sets in her books *Invitations, Celebrations* and *Connections*.[14]

## Folktales

> Three golden apples fell from heaven. . .
> one for the storyteller,
> one for the listener,
> and one for the one who heard.
>
> Armenian folksaying

No matter how ancient a story or folktale, it is not an archeological relic, but a living thing, subject to mutation. Tales are as likely to have grown as to have shrunk. They are glimpses into a particular time, recreating a culture's then current mores. They may have acquired more significance as they pass through time, or they may have been rubbed smooth.

Many such tales have been carried by immigrants to remote parts of the world. Thousands of stories have become a part of the repertoire of many tellers of tales. Once all tales were told and listened to by the unlettered, but beginning five or six thousand years ago, the scribe and his writings began to influence the tradition. The oral teller and his audience were of primary importance, however, and it is through them that these thousands of stories have spread so widely over thousands of miles, favorites both of children and of those who never grow old.

This body of narrative tradition developed gradually, coming from many sources and taking many forms. Often the only versions we have are from literature. Certain authors have retold these tales in their own literary idioms and sometimes they have almost obliterated the original stories. Today's audience will never know how the ancient storytellers told them.

The old stories were transmitted and changed by time and by the times, by the teller and by the listeners, by the country in which they arose, and by the countries to which they were carried. The old tales were changed in the way culture itself changes. "As you follow a story through its changes, you follow the trade routes, the slave routes, the route of a conquering army or that of a restless people on the move. In the beginning, there was the oral tradition, but once writing was established, the written word worked its own magic on 'story' ", according to Jane Yolen.

The transcriber of the tale reshaped old materials but stayed within the limits of the traditional story. The literary folktale is modern and ancient at once, and it was born written. An example would be Joan Aiken's *The Moon's Revenge*, in which she uses the patterns and motifs of long-ago tales: "There was once a boy named Sep who was the seventh son of a seventh son." Folktales are real, however. Taken all together, they offer examinations of human traits, a general explanation of life, a proof of humanity.

Yolen says there are over five hundred known versions of "Cinderella" for all ages and audiences, told and handed down for centuries. "Joseph Jacobs once said about a Cinderella story he printed: 'It was an English version of an Italian adaptation of a Spanish translation of a Latin version of a Hebrew translation of an Arabic translation of an Indian original.'"[15] Each reteller brings to the telling something of his cultural orientation. Is the Chinese admiration for the tiny foot preserved in the Cinderella tale, or is it the seventeenth-century preoccupation with dressing for the ball? Did translations of Charles Perrault's version of the story of the slipper change the Cinderella story for all time, since "de vair" means of fur or ermine, and "de verre" means of glass.

There are now selections, collections, translations, and illustrations for every age and experience in society. A single folktale that has inspired endless listening over the centuries motivates graphic artists such as Maurice Sendak and Michael Foreman to illustrate them.

Folktales are the bare bones of stories; they allow each individual to imagine and add details to the narrative. They say so much in so few words and they are easy to carry in the mind.

Folk literature includes songs, ballads, plays, dances, jokes, superstitions, skipping rhymes, tongue twisters, charms, omens, riddles, games, verses, nursery rhymes, proverbs, fables, parables, tall tales, urban tales, fairy tales, anecdotes, epics, myths, legends, and bible stories.

Stories of today are built on stories from the past. There is no shame in this borrowing.

The author/illustrator Steven Kellogg has retold several larger-than-life legends that beg to be read aloud, alongside the wonderful illustrations that fill the page with visual stories. His picture books about Pecos Bill, Johnny Appleseed, and Paul Bunyan strengthen our concept of tales to retell, of creating personal versions, and the colors, movement, and humor of his paintings will fill children's minds with storying power.

Susan Jeffers builds a fairy tale theme of her own for all ages. Her breathtaking paintings draw special meanings from stories told over centuries, and children hear the words and see the pictures and begin to create their own enchanted versions of these folktales. The artist has brought her own interpretations to the text, and children can lose themselves in the crystal palaces, and find themselves in the classroom full of the memories of their journey, waiting to be shared. Look at her renderings of "The Snow Queen", "Cinderella", and "Thumbelina".

All modern writers write about themselves, just as storytellers of old passed on stories that spoke to them and revealed images of themselves. A story can be read on many levels: a child reads it on one, an adult on another. The creators of modern literary tales for the young must recognize that the child takes the tale "to heart". The writer is the wise one to all children who read what is written: borrowed tales, transcribed tales, literary folktales. G.K. Chesterton writes:

> If you really read the fairy tales, you will observe that one idea runs from one end of them to the other: the idea that peace and happiness can only exist on some condition, an idea which is the core of ethics, the core of the folktale.[16]

Modern tales, borrowing characters and cadences from the folktale, reflect both the individual and society. Stories come out of and then go back into society, changing the shape of that society in turn, and modern myth-makers must not bear this burden lightly. Jane Yolen states that, "A story about a Prince would be historical. A story about a frog would be biological. But a story about a frog Prince is magical."[17] The storyteller is an artist, and selection is essential for art. There are thousands of characters, of details, of motifs. It takes great skill to choose. Ancient humans took in the world mainly by listening — the world was shaped by the oral traditions. The rememberers were the most attuned listeners: the poets, the storytellers, the shamans, and the soothsayers. The carriers of the oral tradition were honored. The early tales and stories from childhood came from asking questions similar to those that children ask, and the best answers of the shamans, the storytellers, and the seers were collected in the oral channel until they reached print.

A tale well told forces a confrontation with the deepest kind of reality, giving the child a focus, the very taste of primary truth. Was the tale made centuries ago, or yesterday? The best of the stories touch the past and the present in all of us.

Folktales, "the stories of the tribe", provide strong reading and listening materials for children. The context of "long ago" enables children to explore all the universal problems and concerns that have troubled humanity forever, but in a safe, non-threatening framework. The deeds of heroes, the schemes of tricksters, the lore of nations past, can all serve as settings for children's own development — family situations, societal difficulties, supernatural beliefs, natural phenomena. They tell "horrifying stories of cannibal kings, and ogres on mountain tops and trolls under bridges who cracked bone and sucked marrow."[18]

Traditional literature — folk and fairy tale, myth and legend from all over the world and ranging from ancient civilizations to twentieth-century emerging nations — makes an excellent starting point for stories. Beautifully illustrated editions of myth, legend, and folk and fairy tale have flooded the market in recent years. For the busy teacher who has little time left to pore over volumes of collected tales, these illustrated versions have been a blessing. (Unfortunately, there has also been a tendency among publishers to stick with a "sure bet", so it's not unusual to find the same familiar stories being illustrated again and again.) Often stories from out-of-print collections such as *The Girl and the Moon Man* by Jeanette Winter, new translations of older material as in the new version of *British Folk Tales* by Kevin Crossley-Holland, unique retellings, illustrating of familiar stories or reinterpretations of traditional material like Fiona French's *art deco* version of *Snow White in New York* are brought dynamically to our attention. One such outstanding example is Brock Cole's *The Giant's Toe*. This is a highly imaginative reworking of *Jack and the Beanstalk* and one destined to take its place alongside Raymond Briggs's wonderful parody, *Jim and the Beanstalk*.

The fun of such retellings lies in the comparisons it invites. Other like sources and variations become the stuff of much speculation and detective work. Did Brock Cole get his idea about losing a toe in a vegetable patch from this old tale in Richard Chase's *American Folk Tales and Songs*?

THE BIG TOE

One time a little boy was hoein' 'taters. He was mad. He liked 'taters 'n beans for supper all right, but there wasn't any meat to put in the beans and he liked *meat* in *his* beans.

Well, he was hackin' with his hoe at a big weed when all-at-once somethin' scrambled under the dirt and went

"UR-R-R-R-R!"

— like it was hurt, and then it went off down under the ground like a big mole. The boy looked and there, lyin' in the dirt, was a big toe. He'd hacked off that somethin's' big toe. He grabbed it up and ran for life! Tore open a few bean vines, knocked down several cornstalks, and jerked the button off the gate gettin' away from there. He made it to the house. Washed that big toe with a dipperful of water and put it in his overall pocket.

And when his Mommy was cookin' supper in the fireplace he eased up the potlid when she had her back turned and slipped that big toe in with the beans. So, when they got to the table and started eatin', that boy ate three big baits of beans — and in one of 'em his Mommy had scooped up that big toe. So he ate it.

Fin'lly his Mommy got the dishes washed and the pots scoured and out the way, and his Daddy got in a load of firewood to cook breakfast, and the boy got in his pile of kindlin' wood, and then they were all sittin' around the fireplace with a lightwood know burnin'. The boy's Mommy she sat on one side, and his Daddy sat on the other, and that boy he was sittin' cross-legged right in the middle of the hearthrock pokin' in the ashes with the poke-stick. And — all at once they heard somethin' 'way off —

"Wha wow woo woe!"

They sat right still, listenin'. Then they heard it again. It was comin' closer.

"Where mow wow woe!"

The boy's Daddy jumped up and barred the door. They sat on sort of wonderin' and sort of scared — and then they heard it out in the road and comin' right that way!

"Where's my big toe?"

The boy's Mommy she jumped up and rolled under the bed, and his Daddy ran and crawled right in after her. They laid there a-shakin' and a-shiverin' so it rattled the bed-slats.

That little boy was so scared he *couldn't* move! Just sat there froze to the hearthrock. Then the gatechain rattled and he heard that thing crunchin' up the path.

"Where's my big to-o-o-o-oe?"

Heard it climbin' up on the porch roof — scratched on up the shingles till it was on top of the house.

"Where's my big to-o-o-o-oe?"

Then it hollered right down the chimney.

"Where's-my-big-TO-O-O-O-O-OE?"

The little boy saw soot fallin', and he looked up, and there, sittin' on the smoke-shelf was a great-big-old-black-hairy Booger. Had big red eyes, big black bushy tail, big claws, and great long sharp snag-teeth. Says, "Where's-my-big-TO-O-O-O-OE? —

YOU GOT IT!"[19]

And did Ian Serraillier write his poem from the memories of an old ballad that shares a similar theme?

THE VISITOR

A crumbling churchyard, the sea and the moon;
The waves had gouged out grave and bone;
A man was walking, late and alone. . .
He saw a skeleton on the ground;
A ring on a bony finger he found.

He ran home to his wife and gave her the ring.
"Oh where did you get it?" He said not a
    thing.

"It's the loveliest ring in the world," she said,
As it glowed on her finger. They slipped off to
    bed.

At midnight they woke. In the dark outside,
"Give me my ring!" a chill voice cried.

"What was that, William? What did it say?"
"Don't worry, my dear. It'll soon go away."

"I'm coming!" A skeleton opened the door.
"Give me my ring!" It was crossing the floor.

"What was that, William? What did it say?"

"Don't worry, my dear. It'll soon go away."

"I'm reaching you now! I'm climbing the bed."
The wife pulled the sheet right over her head.

It was torn from her grasp and tossed in the air.
"I'll drag you out of bed by the hair!"

"What was that, William? What did it say?"
"Throw the ring through the window! THROW IT
    AWAY!"

She threw it. The skeleton leapt from the sill,
Scooped up the ring and clattered downhill,
Fainter . . . and fainter . . . Then all was still.[20]

Some folktales you might like to consider:

*The Enchanted Tapestry*, by Robert San Souci
*Flossie and the Fox*, by Patricia McKissack
*A Japanese Fairy Tale*, by Jane Hori Ike and Baruch Zimmerman
*Mister Cat-and-a-half*, by Richard Pevear
*The Name of the Tree*, by Celia Barker Lottridge
*Princess Gorilla and a New Kind of Water*, by Verna Ardema
*The Story of Wali Dad*, by Kristina Rodanas.

The teacher can incorporate folktale into the curriculum in a variety of ways:
- Take a survey of the kinds of tales the children want to hear about a specific culture: humorous stories, stories about growing into adulthood, stories about aging and death.
- Tell the children a story rather than read it. How does the story change? How do the children react?
- Read aloud a picture-book version of a folktale to the children. What interpretation has the artist placed on the story? What time and culture frame have been created? What values have been added or elaborated upon?
- Have the children design the setting for a tale you are going to read or tell; for example, are we shepherds on a hill, shivering in the cold? Are we in a clearing in a tropical rain forest in Africa?
- Children can bring in other forms of folklore, such as riddles, tongue twisters, recordings, skipping rhymes, chants.
- An integrated arts day may be held at the end of a folklore

unit, including storytelling, folk-art display, puppet plays, songs, games, traditional foods.
- The children can watch a film of a folktale, discussing the film-maker's interpretation of the story.
- The children can retell or record stories they have heard from other relatives or friends. These stories can then be transcribed into literary form.

## Picture Books

The picture book presents an exciting opportunity for engaging children in contextual learning — not "talking about" but "being involved within". The words and pictures work together to synthesize a new creation which appeals especially to today's visually oriented children. The age of the children seems almost irrelevant; the well-chosen picture book embodies those qualities of story and image that draw the child's own experience to the page and let the child see and hear new meanings, negotiating between the child's own world and the world of the author/illustrator. If a group of children takes part in a shared reading/listening activity with a picture book, and if the children subsequently explore, exchange, and clarify ideas and meanings through talk and movement, a learning situation develops that allows for maximum experiencing, and the children make sense not only of the individual responses to a book, but of each other's worlds. Picture books open up opportunities for discussion and therefore deepen understanding; the pictures draw the eye and the text catches the imagination.

In choosing picture books, it is essential to select stories with strong narratives. Folktales or contemporary stories with folk quality help the children travel to another time — an imagined past, an analogous present, an anticipated future. The words can offer powerful language input for the child, story vocabulary, new and varied syntactic patterns, strong contextual clues for exploring meaning, characters who struggle with life's problems — sometimes symbolic, sometimes very real. With such stories, the children are engaged in experiencing language more complex than their own.

Whether the books are labeled picture books or illustrated books, their pictures provide visual input for the child, even for the non-reader. Picture books run the gamut of styles and techniques — watercolors, woodcuts, lithography, photography, and collage; they illuminate the text; they extend the words into possibilities of meaning; they shock the reader/listener with new interpretations, lifting the child's own experience into different conceptual realms. The old is made new; the new is made relevant; the negotiation for the child begins. The picture book is a demanding medium, especially for older readers.

As the artist has brought a personal reality to the words, so children can interpret the meanings of the art individually and collectively. The pictures do not hamper or imprison creative thought; rather, they give structure to energy; they lift the children's ideas, offering patterns for beginnings, suggestions for bouncing against; they present shape, line, color, and proportions as hooks for contrast and comparison. The very difference in the child's view of what is read, heard, and then seen enables the child to see that difference for what it is, the stimulus for looking at one's own particular universe with new eyes. Children can create their pictures in time and space, using active drama techniques, just as a fresh author/illustrator may take the story and present an entirely new concept through graphic design.

By definition, a wordless book holds no difficulties for non-readers or beginning readers. The narrative strength lies in the visuals, and children have the opportunity to provide their own story line, dialogue, and characterization. Imagine the retelling possibilities. The visual literacy that grows from these books will give young readers strength in thought and imagination, and encourage participation in the book experience.

A child's reading strength is dependent upon his or her experiences, both in life and in print. Adults, by sharing picture books with children on their laps or with a group near them, can bring alive the words while, at the same time, the children make sense of the pictures or illustrations. Together word and image blend to make meaning, and the sharing of child and adult as they experience a book builds a special bond that will strengthen the reading process. There are picture books of every type that will meet the needs of particular children. While picture books generally are not read by children, they provide print experience that will lead to independent reading.

Like some films, a picture book can be a pleasure for an

audience spanning a wide age range. Just as *Mary Poppins, Swiss Family Robinson,* and *Star Wars* can be viewed by the whole family, children in the middle years can share in the delight of the picture book and experience stories, memoirs, concepts, and dreams as interpreted by authors and artists using photographs, collage, etches, oils, watercolor, and other media. The text within a picture book must be written concisely and with the art in mind, so that children gain from it a particular and effective communication package. Since picture books were designed to be read aloud, children can experience the literature through both the ear and the eye, and perhaps be touched by the emotional quality inherent in this art-form.

The picture book speaks to most children. It speaks to the child in all of us. Its origins are in cave paintings, in tapestries, in the stories of stained-glass windows. The drama helps the children see those paintings with stronger eyes and critical minds.

What follows is a brief list of some excellent picture books to start you off.

## The Boy of the Three-Year Nap, by Diane Snyder

This is a new adaptation of a traditional Japanese tale which has about it the aura of the "trickster tale". In this instance the trickster's mother gets the upper hand and the tables are turned. We are left wondering, though, whether "a leopard can ever really change its spots". Will the merchant live to regret his new son-in-law? Does the central figure of this story hold up to other famous tricksters such as Anansi?

## The Boy with Two Shadows, by Margaret Mahy

In some old folktales, unfortunate individuals found themselves saddled with terrifying creatures from the world of the supernatural through no fault of their own. Without special help or knowledge the results would be tragic for the victims. Margaret Mahy brings just such a situation into a contemporary setting and saddles a sensitive and caring young boy with the responsibility of looking after a witch's shadow. The shadow is menacing and mean. The boy has only his own resourcefulness to call upon in order to handle the ordeal. The book is never grotesque; the story is handled sensitively. Lots of questions are raised, lots of talk is sure to ensue.

*Hope's Gift*, by Catherine Brighton

Set in the sixteenth century, *Hope's Gift* tells the story of a special child living in the midst of a company of traveling actors. Hope may be a slow child, but she possesses the gift of healing . . . a gift she must not exploit.

*Moses in the Bulrushes*, by Warwick Hutton

The birth and infancy of Moses is retold simply in Hutton's beautiful watercolors. What distinguishes this retelling is the human face that is put on the story. Glimpses of everyday life in ancient Egypt bring this part of the great saga of Israel closer to the contemporary reader.

What Hutton has done with visual storytelling might be compared with Peter Dickinson's unusual perspectives in Old Testament stories in *City Of Gold*.

*Tenrec's Twigs*, by Bert Kitchen

Bert Kitchen's wonderfully realistic paintings of animals from central and south Africa are matched by his simple, gentle story of a Tenrec (a species currently threatened with extinction) who seeks reassurance from the larger animals and birds around him, that his twig building activities are not in vain. In some respects this story has echoes of Jenny Wagner's haunting tale of *The Bunyip of Berkeley's Creek*.

*Where the Forest Meets the Sea*, by Jeannie Baker

An ecological issue — the potential threat to the Australian rain forest — is quietly raised in this gentle, visually alive picture book.

Ms Baker's amazing collages form the setting for this contemporary tale of an outing by a boy and his father to the rain forest. Although set in the present, the hints of past existences are everywhere. The final collage points at what the future could hold for this stunningly beautiful area. Certainly an ideal book for drama work and much further reading, not to mention tremendous possibilities for visual arts work.


## Story Poems

Some poems spin tales and report on people, places, and events, all done with the ear and the eye of the artist. Poets have stories to tell.

Long before most people could read or write, stories and tales were remembered through ballads and songs. Longer story poems used to be more popular than they seem to be today. The rhyme and the rhythm of the poetic form helped to shape the story, and offered help in remembering it. For these reasons, story poems are often effective for choral speaking and dramatizing. Some story poems are built around plot; others have stories hidden beneath the lines. Sometimes the story lies only in the mind of the poet or the listener.

Today, poetry anthologies and song books abound, and teachers can choose from all types to satisfy their particular interests. Some of these books are beautifully illustrated, while others depend upon the strength of the imagination. Authors and song-writers select past favorites (often adapting or rewriting them), use well-known patterns on which to build new ideas, and create wonderful new sounds and images to delight children "through the ear". The language structures and vocabulary that are embedded in poem and song offer a hoard of word power for future meaning-making with print.

Beginning with the success of Shel Silverstein, there has been an explosion of poetry for children. The humor, pathos, and wonder that can be created in a few words seem to represent perfectly the needs of many youngsters. Successful poets know both the interests and the nature of children, and they evoke significant and emotional responses that may surprise adults. Freed from the rhythms and rhymes of jingles and verses, the writers explore all types and formats of poetry, and the children are able to join the word play because there is intellectual and emotional satisfaction in it.

A love of sound is indispensable to a love of words, and what better source of tuning in to sounds of language can there be than the nursery rhyme? Furthermore, the sounds are embodied in materials that tell brief, memorable stories of high interest.

JOHN BOATMAN

Call John the boatman,
Call, call again.

For loud flows the river
And fast falls the rain.
John is a good man, and sleeps very sound;

His oars are at rest and his boat is aground.
Fast flows the river so rapid and deep;
The louder you call him, the sounder he'll
    sleep.

*Tail Feathers from Mother Goose*

This is but one example of subject matter that ranges from comedy to hate, from love and mystery to fantasy:

White bird featherless
Flew from Paradise
Pitched on the castle wall;
Along came Lord Landless
Took it up handless
And rode away horseless
to the King's white hall.

*Ibid.*[21]

From such seemingly simple beginnings, nursery rhymes point children toward stories from all times and traditions.

Doing some research in illustrated nursery rhyme collections can offer a different approach. Now the search for the story will shift to the illustrator's art. What stories have artists like Arnold Lobel or Raymond Briggs drawn from the words?

Perhaps one of the most appealing features of nursery rhyme stories is the form in which they appear. Many of them are miniature scripted dramas with parts indicated for two or more voices.

Children, children, where have you been?
Granny Grey, we've been to London to visit the
    Queen.
What did she give you?
A loaf of bread as big as our head,
A piece of cheese as big as our knees,
A lump of jelly as big as our belly.
Where's my share?
Up in the air.

How shall I get it?
Stand on a chair.
What if I fall?
We don't care.

Traditional

In some cases, there are fragments of ancient signing games, verses left behind from long-forgotten ballads, tag ends of rituals, and patches of song. All offer wonderful opportunities for speaking aloud, building reinterpretation.

It can also be very interesting to compare these little scripts with those created by modern poets. A poem by Michael Rosen demonstrates this with a powerful sense of the way we use language in everyday contexts:

SHUT YOUR MOUTH WHEN YOU'RE EATING

Shut your mouth when you're eating.
    I am, Dad.
MOUTH!
    It is shut
I can see it isn't. I can hear it isn't.
    What about his mouth? You can see every-
    thing in his mouth.
He's only two. He doesn't know any better.
    You can see all his peas and tomato sauce.
That's none of your business.

(2 MINUTES GO BY)
    Dad.
Yes.
    Your mouth's open. Shut your mouth when
    you're eating.
It is shut, thank you very much.
    I can see it isn't, Dad. I can see all the food
    in there.
Look that's my business, OK?
    Peas, gravy, spuds, everything.
Look, you don't want to grow up to be as horri-
    ble as your father do you? Answer that, smar-
    tyboots.[22]

Rosen's scripted monologues and dialogues are so close to the lives of most children that speaking them aloud seems entirely natural. In fact, timing, pacing, intonation, and rhythm are caught almost instantly. The children's own verse from street and playground can also be examined and compared with the work of poets and with older works from the oral tradition.

Moving through and about this great medley of sound and voice and rhythm and story cannot help but keep the sounds of language ringing forever in the ears of the children we teach.

The following demonstrates how one class probed deeper into Judith Nicholls's "Moses . . . A sequence".

Before introducing the poem, the teacher read from the Old Testament the story of Moses and the exodus from Egypt. She asked the children to be aware of any five things that made a pattern. At the conclusion of the reading, the children made lists of patterns they had discovered. For example, some made lists of magical transformations (e.g., burning bush, staff to serpent, water to blood), others made lists of water imagery. The children were then asked to explain the "big idea" behind their patterns.

Using an overhead projector, the teacher introduced the five poems that comprise "Moses . . . A sequence". After the children had opportunities to read the poems silently and out loud, they attempted to figure out the big idea behind Nicholls's pattern. They settled on groups of speakers, each telling an aspect of the Moses story from unique points of view. To test their ideas, each poem was assigned to a group whose task was to bring to life the voice of the speaker, and to convey in the oral reading both the intended audience and the purpose for telling the story.

Here is the first poem in the sequence:

SEARCHER

Princess, what are you dreaming,
down among the moist rushes?
Soft pleated linen, beaded bracelets,
purple grapes and Pharaoh's finest wines
await you at the palace —
yet you follow
a wavering baby's cry[23]

The group working with this selection settled on the voices of ladies-in-waiting, gossiping among themselves in the bulrushes as they observed Pharaoh's daughter following the cries of the baby Moses. Hushed voices and mocking tones were employed to put this across.

Interpretation of the other pieces ranged from work songs of laborers told in call-and-response fashion to games played by children to a cast rehearsal of a play celebrating the crossing of the Red Sea by descendants of those ancient Israelites.

For these children, the saga of Israel became just that, and by approaching story in this way, the children were learning that storytelling is as much about how the story is shaped as it is about what happened to whom and why.

The more they talked about it, thought about it, and revisited it, the greater became their awareness of the incredible energy and power that stories possess.

It is important to foster openness to story and to avoid activities that seek to regulate and control. Talking about the images we see, listening to the musical sounds we hear, and retaining some idea of what we think the story is telling us should be central to our work with storytelling in the classroom. If this is so, the problems of bringing story poems to life will turn into a real adventure. At the same time, our memories of the stories we have worked with will have been enriched by the involvement of our community of classroom storytellers.

Some story poems are short:
*The Word Party*, by Richard Edwards

Some are long:
*The Mighty Slide*, by Allan Ahlberg

Some are built around plot:
*Borrowed Black: A Labrador Fantasy*, by Ellen Bryan Obed

Others have stories hidden beneath the lines:
*Night Cars*, by Teddy Jam and Eric Beddows

Some are beautifully illustrated:
*The Wheels on the Bus*, by Maryann Kovalski

Others depend on the strength of the imagination: *Boo to a Goose*, by John Mole

## Novels

Children possess a great range of reading abilities, and their common need is to read widely and often. There must be a large selection of books for those children who are moving into independent reading, but who may not have much security with print, who need high motivation accompanied by material that is accessible. It is a good book that pulls a child into the story so that he or she wants to read it completely, to feel the satisfaction and pleasure that a good book gives. Books that are written with a controled vocabulary and simplistic art will seldom make a child want to read.

Children gain reading power through in-depth experiences with novels. Truly great authors seem to understand the needs of children, and there are many fine books from which to choose. Children enjoy reading several books by a favored author, or a series of books about a familiar set of characters. Common themes link the most widely read books — humor, school friends, mystery, fantasy — and children should be given as many opportunities as possible for reading independently. Boys and girls may prefer different types of books, and yet there are fine novels that, if brought to their attention, will fill their interest needs and present non-sexist portrayals.

For those children who have developed into mature, independent readers, there are many novels they will enjoy reading which, while written at an appropriate print and emotional level, challenge their concepts and ideas. Rather than moving to "harder" or more adult fiction, these children need to deepen their reading experiences, moving into quality alongside quantity. Novels from other countries, such as Alicia Hilary Ruben's *The Calf of the November Cloud*; other cultures, such as Geraldine Kaye's *Comfort Herself*; or other contexts, such as *The Snow Spider* by Jenny Nimmo, can present young readers with problems and situations of greater complexity, subtle characterization, and multifaceted plot structures. Children can read the novels that represent the best in fiction for them.

For generations, children have enjoyed a body of novels that seem never to age or date. Because of the universal truths that hold constant, children can read or listen to books that portray a different life from their own, in custom, place, time, or circumstance — for instance, E. Nesbit's *The Story of the Amulet* or Leon Garfield's *Smith*. For some children, these differences make the reading difficult, and the stories may have to be read to them.

Novels for young adolescents allow readers to engage in a dialogue with an author on a wide range of topics and at a deep, emotional level. The themes of these novels reflect the development of young adolescents, their concern about their place in the adult world, ecology, peace, the future, and the past. Adults must understand the need these young readers have to understand life's problems, and accept that the portrayal and careful and artful examination of issues within the novel form will help consolidate and clarify the values and beliefs of young people.

For many children, novels provide road maps for the difficulties of contemporary life, and they identify and live through the exploits of the fictitious characters they read about. Through themes, adults can help children deal with specific concerns via a range of novels that meet their wants and needs.

The teacher can work with novels that children have read as a class, that a group has read, different novels on a theme, or a novel that has been read aloud to the class over a period of time. As well, the teacher can set up storying activities that prepare a class for a novel, or read the novel alongside the class. A novel contains a wealth of stories inside, and will promote through response dozens of others.

The following is an example of how one teacher approached a very challenging novel with a group of sixteen-year-olds. The novel, *A Parcel of Patterns* by Jill Paton Walsh, deals with the struggles of the residents of the English village of Eyam to fight the Black Plague during the latter half of the 1600s. It is a tale of collective heroism as the residents, hoping to contain the ravages of the plague, vow to remain in their own village no matter what. The work bears amazing echoes of the struggle to contain the AIDS virus that threatens our own age.

The novel itself sets up some interesting challenges for the reader. First, there are no distinct chapter divisions. The work proceeds through patterns of stories weaving in and among themselves. There is, for example, the story of the village, its time, and its character. There is the story of Mall Percival, the central narrator. There is the story of two parsons. There is the story of beliefs, customs, and rituals of the time. There is the story of the rich and the poor, and there is the story about storytelling, for in their attempts to fight the plague, the villagers lean heavily on three kinds of stories. First, the word of God as explained to them by their parsons; second, the words of their ancestors as contained in their folk sayings and rituals; and third, the stories that they make and tell each other about the plague as they see it.

Added to this is the manner of speaking that characterized Puritans living at the time. A terrific challenge and well worth it, every bit.

The teacher in this case realized that here was a book that would require a good portion of time building up high levels of anticipation. In order to waste no time capturing his students' attention, he decided to use a technique that film-makers have employed for years to whet interest. He would first "preview" the work by plunging his students right into the middle of it.

The reading commenced at the following point in the text:

Now word was out it was the Plague we had; such secrets do not keep for long. Folk took fright at it. On the morrow of the day when my mother had been offended at Parson Momphesson's counsel, we were awoken from our beds by such a clattering and to-do in the street as we had seldom heard; and going to the casements and brushing off the breath-dew upon the glass, we saw three empty carts going up the town. As we took breakfast there came a neighbour to tell us that they were gone up to Sheldon's Farm; and ere we were done eating the carts came down again, laden high with chests and chairs and bundles, and the baby strapped on the top of the curtain-bale, crying loud, and manservants and maidservants carrying, or driving cows, and the little boy Sheldon leading the goat, and Mistress Sheldon bearing in her arms a loudly quacking hamper of withy-weave. Even the ducks from the pond were going away!

As you may well suppose, this noise and spectacle

brought families staring into every doorway in the road; and they had their fill of it too, for at the tail of the procession came Mistress Agnes Sheldon, Farmer Sheldon's spinster sister, a deal older than he and a thorn in his flesh daily, as all the world well knew. And as she walked she railed upon him.

'Going to Hazleford, indeed!' she cried. Since when was Hazleford grand enough for Sheldons, may I ask?'

'Thou hadst best hold thy tongue, and come too, sister,'' said Farmer Sheldon.

'Fie upon you, brother, for a cowardly man! What will the neighbours think?' cried she. And, lest we didn't think what she supposed, she continued, 'I'll tell thee — they'll wonder what evil deed is on thy conscience, brother, that thou art afraid of the Lord's vengeance! An honest man fears not the Plague, but trusts in God! Oh, thou shameful fellow, thou . . .'

'Go to, sister, go to,' he said, hanging down his head. And by now half the town was trotting along behind the trundling carts, and the shouting woman, all ears and smiles. My mother and I went along with all the rest; my father had more dignity, but he missed the best of it.

Beside the churchyard gate she baited him at last to stand at bay. 'There is a foul contagion here,' he said. 'And we are going to a place of clean airs and safety until it has passed. And, sister, I implore thee for thy own health to come with us . . .'

'He hath another farm at Hazleford,' she told the eager crowd, 'which ever till now my lady his wife thought not fit for her — though she hath tried very hard to make me dwell in it — and now, lo! suddenly it is good enough and more. Bad conscience, bad conscience, say I! That baggage his wife hath cause to fear the Lord's displeasure, and dare not say that the righteous shall fear no ill, not she!'

'Oh, sister, for shame!' said poor Mistress Sheldon, very red. 'Thou knowest no ill of me, that you should speak of me thus.'

'Dost thou think the Lord sees not what way you treat a poor spinster aunt?' cried she. 'Dost thou think the Lord knows not what happened to my silver thimble, or who tore my stump-work box? Did not the Lord hear thee, yesterday se'ennight, what thou saidst to me?'

We overhearers were all moved to laughter, and that intemperately, till our sides would split; but, sudden, here was the old Parson Stanley, coming down the street to us.

'Agnes Sheldon,' said he, very grave and severe, 'the Lord's displeasure is not thine to bandy with. Thou dost blaspheme. Silent, woman!'

A small gleam of triumph entered the eye of the farmer's wife, and she darted a glance at her terrible sister-in- law but said not a word . . .[24]

The students read the excerpt silently. They were encouraged to jot down any thoughts, reactions, or questions that occurred to them.

Next, in pairs, each told the other what they had visualized as the incident unfolded.

The whole class came together to share their images. Some students had very sharp pictures in their minds. "I saw the baby's head bobbing on top of the furniture piled on the cart." Others had less clear images, but had a feeling of the moment, like a sort of hazy pencil sketch or line drawing. Still others reported being aware of their own physical relationship to the scenes they witnessed. "I was inside a house, peeking out through an opening in the curtains."

When they had nearly exhausted their thoughts, the teacher directed the students to reread the excerpt, paying particular attention to moments of conflict.

The students formed small groups after the reading and, acting on the teacher's instructions, chose one conflict to reproduce for readers' theatre. Because this excerpt dealt with a crowd, the students were encouraged to build some improvisation in and around the segments to be read. For most groups, this translated into crowd reaction to the reader's words.

Each group took turns reading its prepared scene to at least one other group.

The whole class reconvened, and the teacher discussed with the students the difficult decision Farmer Sheldon had taken. The children were then asked to anticipate additional decisions that they thought the characters in the novel might face. At the conclusion of this discussion, each student was asked to write a diary entry in the role of a villager who described one of these difficult decisions.

Finally, the class divided into groups of five. One member of each group was to be an artist, the others his or her models. The groups were asked to create a "living painting" that informed the class about the lives of ordinary people living in Eyam during the plague.

The artists and their subjects used their diary entries for their ideas, then tableaux were shaped under each artist's direction.

The session concluded with the viewing of each "living painting" as the artist explained to the viewers the artistic decisions that had been made in putting across the ideas.

Copies of the novel were now distributed to the eager hands stretched out in excitement and anticipation.

Stories sometimes leave us puzzled — questions are unanswered or resolutions do not fit our frame of reference. Stories also beget stories. Many personal experiences of the reader come bubbling to the surface, demanding to be heard. All of this is rich in possibilities for future action. Thus it is that after the story, time is needed to consider our own thoughts and to become aware of the thinking of those around us.

There is still too much emphasis in schools on student answering of pre-set questions after the reading of a story. Such practice short-circuits the response mode by switching attention to what should be known about a story, rather than encouraging students to pose their own questions and make their own statements. It is through the development of genuine inquiry that our students learn. They must have their own chances to seek and solve problems. Novels present complex stories for exploration.

Here are some examples:

*Children of the Wolf*, by Jane Yolen
A fascinating novel conjured up from actual documents that describe the feral, wild children of India in the 1920s.

*Dear Mr. Henshaw*, by Beverly Cleary
A story told though a series of letters, and then through a personal diary, by a young boy learning to cope with parents and the complexities of growing up.

*Dogsong*, by Gary Paulsen
A powerful story of an Innuit boy's ice floe walkabout, a journey of physical and spiritual self-discovery.

*The Haunting*, by Margaret Mahy
This New Zealand writer creates a masterful ghost story about Barney, a boy who is afraid to tell about the messages he receives from a dead relative.

*Shadow in Hawthorn Bay*, by Janet Lunn
A young girl in nineteenth-century Scotland travels to Canada after having a mysterious premonition that her cousin is in trouble. When she arrives, she discovers that the cousin is dead and she must face winter in the woods alone.

## CHAPTER 4

# Working with Stories

THE OLDER THE VIOLIN THE SWEETER THE TUNE

Me Granny old
Me Granny wise
stories shine like a moon
from inside her eyes

Me Granny can dance
Me Granny can sing
but she can't play the violin.

Yet she always saying,
'Dih older dih violin
de sweeter de tune.'

Me Granny must be wiser
than the man inside the moon.

John Agard[1]

## Listening to the Children

If children are to learn from a story, they must be able to express their individual personal concerns, ideas, and feelings about it, interacting with it on all levels. The teacher's role is to promote thoughtful story response, to empower children to wander inside and wonder about the story, making all kinds of meaning connections, deepening their private and public picture of the words. The classroom can be a place where children can safely explore those connections, with the teacher as champion and lifeguard. The idea is to set up situations where the children can begin negotiating the meanings that relate the story to their lives, the author to the story, the stories that other students build to the stories in their own minds, the words that tell the story to the words that form their lives, the patterns in the story to the grammar in the head, the world of the story to the world of the moment. It is these forged links to learning that make story talk worthwhile.

A school must not demean story by turning it into predigested learning, nor must it turn story into an icon to be worshipped. Instead, story must be for children a good thing to experience, aesthetic and affective first, pleasurable and desirable, familiar and strange, ordinary and fabulous. If we as teachers are concerned with imparting a particular truth about the content of the story, then the story we share is ours, not theirs. When it comes to printed stories, each reader paints his own story picture. Two readers may both read about the author's life, commit the details to memory, and summarize them on a worksheet, but the story I read and the story you read will never completely match.

If we rob children of their own stories in an attempt to make a common story, we render learning insignificant, and we turn pleasure into pain. Our goal of response must be one of deepest learning, not of leading children to solve a puzzle that we have designed and of which we know the outcome. Instead, we must help children through their own story mazes, arming them for battle, nursing their wounds, giving them sustenance, sharing our wisdom. The fight must be theirs and the victory over the Minotaur a ritual of their own literacy.

As story teachers, we do not believe in simplistic responses that demonstrate no thought or growth. However, we must design activities that cause children to read carefully, extend their knowledge, elaborate upon first understanding, invent new patterns of thought. We must not be thought of as "anything goes" teachers, but as rigorous, demanding story masters who make the journey into story possible. Children will respect and respond to story teaching. There is no need to purchase manuals with answers for either teacher or child. Be wary of booklets purporting to lead children into a story by way of creative activities. Children must have a say in how they will respond. They respond individually and then bring their information to the group or the class. If we take the time to listen to ideas, the talk will flow more truly and develop from the needs and wants of the children.

Responding to story is as important as meeting story. Children must be permitted to respond personally and individually, expressing their ideas, feelings, and preferences in many different ways, demonstrating their growth and development in their response patterns, as they talk about the story, retell it, create their own versions, role-play from the story, write about ideas engendered by the story, paint and model characters and events, read more along the story line, read the story dialogue aloud, or celebrate the author of the story. With the teacher's careful intervention, collaborative response can grow from activities that extend the personal response and help generate a wider and more thoughtful appreciation of the story. Teachers must, as Charlotte Huck says, "provide windows on responses."[2]

After children have responded personally to a story, they will begin to explore the more traditional elements of literature — plot, characterization, setting, etc. In our sharing work, we seldom use those terms; rather, the children often bring them up in their own questioning or researching. Making meaning is the goal of storying together, and when terms of reference are useful, they can be explained. Then the knowledge about story grows from need and context.

Not always do we ask for an external response. Sometimes the sharing of the story is a complete experience in itself. Sometimes the children are making meaning from the collective hearing/reading of the story. They may call upon the experience later. There may be no need for external response at the moment. Reflective journals, putting the story into writing, remembering the story at a later date; all are modes of responding that help children build a story frame.

Printed stories require special attention. As teachers we must be conscious of what takes place during the children's acts of reading, their ways of getting at stories, their dependence on certain patterns to structure their interpretation, and the way their views change.

Developing readers — that is, people who pick up books and read willingly because they value the experience — do not materialize overnight. It takes time to build a frame of reference for literature and to become confident as a reader. Indeed, true readers are probably always in a state of "becoming".

For this reason alone, it is crucial that teachers bear in mind the importance of accumulated reading experience and develop a sense of continuity with respect to good practice throughout the years of schooling.

To begin with, the reading environment is going to have to

be carefully considered. It goes without saying that availability of books will be a prime consideration, not just a wide range of types and genres or books from many cultures, but also books that represent what the children have read in the past, old favorites to be dipped into again and again, what they are reading now (current interests), and what they will read in the future (books in which concepts are within the range of understanding, but the language may as yet be a bit difficult. In all probability, these are the books which the teacher will choose to read to the class).

In this setting, children must be offered the freedom to make their own choices and be given generous opportunities to read, to get lost in a book if need be.

Of course, knowing the children and their interests is absolutely essential in providing the material they need. In many instances, great patience and flexibility will be required, for we must, to a certain extent, go in the directions in which the children need to go.

At the same time, the students' own publications must be integrated into the reading and sharing experiences of the classroom. Above all, teachers must be prepared to accommodate a wide range of responses to the reading. Talk, drama, painting, dance, writing, modeling, spontaneous laughter, letters to authors will be but a small part of the outpouring of expression.

A major plank in building a community of readers is the communal sharing of literature which has been discussed earlier. Hand in hand with this activity goes the teacher's own talk about personal reading that he or she enjoys. Teachers who read aloud with enthusiasm, who tell stories that bathe the listeners in the richness of language, are providing models of excellence for their students. When they also share their enthusiasm for their own reading, they reinforce the models.

Listening to children, taking heed of what they tell us about stories, can influence considerably how we teach with stories. Children want a good yarn. They want to be drawn into stories, to be part of them, and at times to identify with them. For example, after listening to Jane Yolen's *The Girl Who Loved the Wind*, one class expressed considerable interest in the servants in the story. Since the servants scarcely figured in the tale, the teacher was puzzled by this response. The children explained that the merchant in the story (the girl's father) was a mean-tempered man. He had lost his daughter to the wind and as far as they were concerned, the servants would bear the brunt of his anger and frustration. The teacher had built a lesson around predicting how the girl would manage in her new life, living with the wind. The children weren't interested. As far as they were concerned, she had escaped living like a virtual prisoner in her father's house and had a new life. It was the fate of those left behind they were concerned about. The teacher quickly picked up on this and the result was a stimulating story adventure. What this illustrates is the need for teachers to take the time to help their students pursue responses. Too often, teachers feel pressed to offer a quick solution or invoke closure. Sometimes, it is as important to pursue the playful and spontaneous as it is to adhere to the teacher-initiated, "serious" direction.

How can you tune in to the children's thinking? Talk about the story is the most obvious way. It is also one that has been much abused. Too often, what passes for talk about a story is merely a question-and-answer exercise which does little to expand the children's ability to respond. Perhaps what needs to be considered are:

- ways and means of helping children to reflect on their ideas in order to give them voice;
- informal avenues for exploration which can be carried out by the children in small groups before discussing with the large group;
- a physical arrangement of the room that encourages participation in a given activity;
- strategies that will encourage peer talk rather than lectures by the teacher;
- strategies that will encourage children to listen to each other and respond to each other's answers by building on them, not evaluating them.

How can we help children become engaged in the life of the story? This is one of the main concerns of teachers who are keen to develop classroom practices which promote a love of story and reading.

Much current thinking on the subject encourages teachers to help their students explore their personal responses through a wide variety of activities. In order to do this, listening to what children consider important about stories and acknowledging what they care about is absolutely essential. Like most readers, children want to discuss what they have enjoyed about a story; they want to explore those aspects of the story implicit in the text and ponder the connections they have made between the story and their own lives and the lives lived in other stories. If children come to associate reading only with someone else's questions, if they have little opportunity to say in their own way what they think and feel, then stories will mean very little to them.

All children require patient listening, one on one, but teachers must work with large groups, and although there will be time for individual conferencing, they must also become alert to the possibilities and opportunities for talking with their classes about stories and working with them.

> The first sentence of every novel should be:
> 'Trust me, this will take time but there is order
> here, very faint, very human.' Meander if you
> want to get to town.
>
> Michael Ondaatje[3]

Dorothy Heathcote once stated that it is the job of the teacher to help learners reveal what they know and to give them the opportunity to care about learning more.[4]

It is our purpose to help teachers do just that by suggesting ways in which they can work with large groups to aid them in their storying:

- maximizing contact with a wide variety of stories from all historical periods and from many cultures and written in different genres and styles;
- helping children understand that stories are forms to be experienced, not artifacts to be studied;
- encouraging play with stories and with the imaginative material the stories provide;
- offering children a variety of ways in which they can give form to their reading experiences;
- helping children to tell the story of their reading and in

so doing, enhancing their ability to handle a variety of texts;

- helping children sharpen their memories of stories they have experienced;
- helping children to mange longer, more intricate stories.

The teacher should be a chaperon, perhaps best contributing by feeding into the discussions references drawn from his or her wider reading experience and book knowledge, helping to add depth and range to what is said.

Jack Thompson says the mutual sharing of reading experiences through conversation is the best method of all by which peer influences can be organized and channeled.[5]

## Inside, Outside, and All Around the Story

Children can engage in the life of a story through four processes:

1. Interpreting the Story (sharing what we have beheld)
   - exploring a story, looking for personal images and group images
   - sticking with the story (close reading)
   - dramatizing the story in role
   - retelling the story
   - reconstructing the story
   - working with the story's patterns, images, or narrative styles

2. Elaborating (building on the story's strengths)
   - burrowing into the story for hidden, unstated truths
   - examining the story, relating it to personal situations
   - looking at story bits and expanding them
   - building story webs based on questions and concerns of the children themselves
   - engaging with the story to make new meanings
   - finding the questions that the children want to explore

3. Extending the Story (stretching the tale)
   - extending the plot before or after the story
   - building upon the group's ideas of what might have happened or what could happen next
   - building on the story's concepts by designing new contexts for it or placing it alongside others

- finding the stories within stories
- problem-solving unresolved situations

4. Inventing from the Story (creating new from old)
   - building a set of stories modeled on the original — using patterns from the story to create new ones
   - using characters from the story in other plot settings
   - using contexts and concepts from the story as the basis for new ones

Harold Rosen says that every story contains within it the seeds of other potential stories, the ghosts of narratives that have given up their lives for the sake of the tale in which they are embedded — the stories exact a ruthless economy.[6] When we write from inside the world of the story, when what we write is dependent upon the original source, we give the child a huge repertoire of resources that he or she can draw upon, and we also give him or her a set of constraints to become aware of. This type of "dependent authorship" lets students look at their own work, at the work of the story, all at once. When we add to the story, continue the story, or write epilogues for the story, or rewrite the ending, the children are involved in shared authorship.

When it comes to sharing stories through reading, the important thing is not so much how many books we have read, but whether reading has been a means of relating the experiences of our lives to those of others. The truth of any story is always limited by what we bring to that story. It is the way in which we reflect on experience and generalize from it that ultimately causes us to modify our behavior, to gain understanding.

There are many ways to set the process in motion, the simplest of these being discussion after reading. Among other things we can also make comparisons with other stories dealing with the same theme, enact the text to explore meanings and interpretations, encourage the children to raise and focus on questions that get at the universal truths that touch all our lives, and by means of dramatic inventing try to relate our understanding of life to those of story characters. The main thing is that we do something with what we read.

Retelling stories is another strategy we can use. It is amazing when we retell narratives how personal our own retellings become. In our own words, we reveal not only the story but ourselves. We alter details, remove some, add others, we make the story our own. It is told from our point of view, telling as much about us as about the story.

We want children to retell with equally imaginative energy. In our work with story we don't want to just invent activities that start with the story and then leave it, we want the children to constantly return and refer to the story, remaking and creating meanings.

> We are the meaning-makers — every one of us: children, parents, and teachers. To try to make sense, to construct stories, and to share them with others in speech and in writing is an essential part of being human. For those of us who are more knowledgeable and more mature — parents and teachers — the responsibility is clear; to interact with those in our care in such a way as to foster and enrich their meaning-making.
>
> Gordon Wells,
> *The Meaning Makers*[7]

## Tackling a Story

In *When Johnny and Judy Don't Read*, Maurice Saxby cautions teachers about "cheap plastic ways of appearing to be involving children with literature."[8] This is a critical issue, and as teachers, we must continually challenge our own work by ensuring that what we are pursuing is something that the children are interested in; that we are not forcibly persuading them to follow our lead, but determining if they might be better off at this point getting on with a self-chosen activity or perhaps another story.

It has already been pointed out that by developing a healthy spirit of inquiry among the children, by encouraging them to become a community interested in seeking and testing ideas, some of the concerns cited above will take care of themselves.

Arthur Yorinks, whose books for children include the 1987 Caldecott-winning *Hey, Al*, indicates something of his own spirit of inquiry in a *New York Times* review of Margaret Mahy's illustrated poem, *17 Kings and 42 Elephants*. Asks Yorinks, "What are those kings? Where are they going? Why are there so many elephants? So many questions bubble up."

He goes on to state his concerns about the illustrations, which are not unappealing, yet "pictures end up as decorations, not illustrations. They do nothing to expand or amplify or resonate the text. There is so much room in those carefully crafted phrases to explore, yet the pictures seem to be just along for the ride. Instead of 'illustrating' the words, where is a subtext, a counterpoint, a punch line to the pictures?"[9]

This subtext, or counterpoint, is precisely what we are dealing with here, and we help the children to think about this by encouraging them to look for the stories inside the story and the storytellers who tell those stories. Since Arthur Yorinks has raised just such questions about *17 Kings and 42 Elephants*, perhaps it will make a good starting point.

> Seventeen kings on forty-two elephants
> Going on a journey through a wild wet night,
>
> Baggy ears like big umbrellaphants,
> Little eyes a-gleaming in the jungle light.
>
> Seventeen kings saw white-toothed crocodiles
> Romping in the river where the reeds grow tall,
>
> Green-eyed dragons, rough as rockodiles,
> Lying in the mud where the small crabs crawl.
>
> Forty-two elephants — oh, what a lot of 'ums,
> Big feet beating in the wet wood shade,
>
> Proud and ponderous hippopotomums
> Danced to the music that the marchers made.
>
> Seventeen kings sang loud and happily,
> Forty-two elephants swayed to the song.
>
> Tigers at the riverside drinking lappily,
> Knew the kings were happy as they marched along.
>
> Who joined the singsong? Cranes and pelicans,
> Pelicans fluttering their fine fantails,
>
> Flamingos chanting "Ding Dong Bellicans!"

Rosy as a garden in the jungle vales.

Tinkling tunesters, twangling trillicans,
Butterflied and fluttered by the great green trees.

Big baboonsters, black gorillicans
Swinging from the branches by their hairy knees.

Kings in crimson, crowns all crystalline,
Moving to the music of a single gong.

Watchers in the jungle, moist and mistalline,
Bibble-bubble-babbled to the bing-bang-bong!

Seventeen kings — the heavy night swallowed them,
Raindrops glistened on the elephants' backs.

Nobody stopped them, nobody followed them —
The deep dark jungle has devoured their
tracks.[10]

Of course, the longer they can linger over the text, the more likely it is that questions will begin to occur to the children. Helping them linger, making it worthwhile lingering, keeping it all interesting is the challenge of our teaching.

Because the poem is so rhythmical and so much fun to speak aloud, unison choral speaking with lots of solos is a natural entry point. After a few practice runs with much revision and sharing of solos, the sound effects of the jungle could be added. Trumpeting elephants, shrieking peacocks, and other sounds of the natural world could be contrasted with human-made sounds — the gong which keeps the entire ensemble together, the voices of singing kings and the slapping feet of the trackers who would most likely be clearing the path in front of the procession.

A sound composition might be of interest, now possibly recreating the jungle prior to the entry of the kings, during their passage, and afterwards.

If enthusiasm for this work is high, it is but a short leap into the inside stories. With as much time as they have spent searching the text for clues to jungle and human sounds, the children are certain to spot clues such as "Watchers in the jungle" and begin considering who witnessed this event and what they thought about it.

Perhaps we can find out who the watchers might have been; what they thought they were seeing; how their lives were altered by the incident; whether they felt threatened or curious or angry. Is this a story of quest, conquest, or celebration? Would it make any difference to our reading if we knew who was telling the story? Perhaps the children can leave this poem with a little more insight, a little more daring, possibly some extraordinary ideas.

Sometimes, inquiry leads us in a different direction, and instead of finding stories inside the story, a new story develops based on an incident, theme, or character from the original. What follows is a description of just such an occurrence with a class of eleven-year-olds. Their teacher had read to them *The Village of Round and Square Houses* by Ann Grifalconi.

It is a true story about the village of Tos, Cameroons, West Africa, which is certainly unique in the world, for the women live in round houses and the men live in square ones. The basis of this arrangement is a story that happened to the ancestors of these people. The story involves the near-extinct volcano near which the village of Tos is situated. Contemporary rituals are an aspect of this story within a story. The remoteness of the village and the incredible difference between life there and in modern western societies is quite fascinating.

At the conclusion of the reading, the children were keen to discuss life in the remote area and to compare their own lives with the lives of children in Tos. In particular, certain daily rituals drew attention.

In order to build on this interest, the teacher asked the children to invent other rituals which they thought might be practised by the villagers of Tos. In the ensuing activity, the children invented several which related to clues they had gleaned from the story. Many of these were connected to the growing and harvesting of food.

The teacher assembled the children and announced, in role, that as a visitor to Tos she had been very impressed with the rituals and was eager to learn more. She then asked each child in turn his or her village name and also what their part had been in the ritual and what it meant to them.

At this point the teacher stopped the role-playing and asked the children to think of some questions they might like to explore with respect to the village of Tos.

The children seemed to be most interested in knowing if villagers were free to leave the village and go into the outside world. If they did do this would they be welcome to return? Could strangers visit?

It was then decided by the children that they wanted to be the outsiders first, planning to visit this village. Eventually they decided that they were scientists sent to prepare the villagers for relocation because it was feared that the volcano near which they lived would erupt again, just as it had centuries before. In groups of five, the children were to decide how they would approach the villagers with this dreadful news. Each group in turn then faced the combined groups, who represented the residents of Tos, and tried to persuade them that they must leave their ancestral lands. No group was successful in persuading the people to uproot themselves and move to a safer location. In the discussion that followed, the children decided that what would be important would be to equip the people to know when danger was imminent and help them to formulate an emergency plan which could be put into action.

Frequently, the children will want to continue a story if the ending doesn't seem completely tidy. It's not so much a new story in such cases as it is a reworking of story elements. In the case of Ed Young's *The Eyes of the Dragon*, a village has been left in ruins because of the stubbornness of the village magistrate. A wall around the village which affords much-needed protection has collapsed, destroying many homes and leaving the villagers in chaos. There are many implications about who is responsible, but the main thing is that the story ends leaving everything in a mess.

In one classroom, the children banded into groups, each group representing one main character in the story. The teacher, in role as an investigator dispatched by the Chinese Emperor, hot-seated each group in an attempt to get to the bottom of the situation and to help the villagers form a rebuilding plan.

The work leaned heavily on the children's recall of actual and imagined events from the story. In the drama process of interviewing the villagers, it was agreed that the rebuilding of the wall should commence immediately. When it came time to decide who would do it, a situation not unlike the story of *The Little Red Hen* emerged. Some within the village, it seemed, were beyond manual labor and only wanted to supervise. Suddenly, a whole new story had developed.

Among the most challenging material to deal with is that which might be described as elliptical. We are given only bits and pieces to work with, but must work with them to try and construct the whole story. In order to get anywhere with this kind of material, lots of inference must be encouraged.

Walter De La Mare's "Song of the Mad Prince" is a good example of a selection that demands a great deal of the reader's thought and imagination in order to find the story.

THE SONG OF THE MAD PRINCE

Who said, 'Peacock Pie'?
The old king to the sparrow:
Who said, 'Crops are ripe'?
Rust to the harrow:
Who said, 'Where sleeps she now?
Where rests she now her head,
Bathed in eye's loveliness?' —
That's what I said.

Who said, 'Aye mum's the word'?
Sexton to willow:
Who said, 'Green dusk for dreams,
Moss for a pillow'?
Who said, 'All time's delight
Hath she for narrow bed;
Life's troubled bubble broken'? —
That's what I said.[11]

In working with children, it is sometimes useful to describe the poem as a bicycle wheel minus the outer rim and with several spokes missing. Our job will be to rebuild the wheel.

After listening to the selection read aloud and then reading it silently, it is useful to engage the children in an oral discussion of the piece. Involving them at the outset in activity makes the selection less intimidating and gives the sounds of the poem lots of time to sink in. The object of the work at this point is not to start explaining the piece, but instead to view it in terms of its possibilities for interpretation aloud.

Perhaps the children could begin by reading antiphonally —

half the class reading the questions, the other half reading the rest of the poem. Then they might read in pairs. They could first try reading from different physical points (e.g., Reader A pretends she is seated behind Reader B in a movie theatre); then attempt different emotional states (Reader A finds the subject matter scary, Reader B finds the material quite matter-of-fact). The readers might adopt roles and read with them in mind. (A is an arrogant queen; B is a humble servant.) Another possibility is to divide the children into small groups and encourage them to invent a game or ritual that accompanies the words (in one classroom, a group treated the piece as a work chant. A foreman called out the question and the laborers chanted the responses in unison as they hauled heavy cargo from a ship).

By now the children are speaking the words with ease, improvising on the rhythms and language patterns and in general displaying much confidence with their reading.

Now perhaps we can read for the voice of the storyteller and attempt to portray the intent behind the story.

The children might focus on the title, and consider what causes people to go mad, then discuss in small groups the overt behavior of people who are mad. Now, instead of treating the selection in question-and-answer fashion with two voices, the groups might be challenged to prepare a group oral reading incorporating their ideas about the voice(s) of madness.

At this point, the children might be asked what questions they would like to ask about the piece. In many instances, the questions tend to focus on key expressions or words — e.g., Who is the old king? What is a harrow? The class might be asked to select some of the word pictures that interest them and to list and discuss them.

Often it helps our understanding of a selection if we can surround it with a set of stories that help us to think about meanings.

For example, a discussion of the old king might bring into focus what we know about old kings from stories. Not all of them are the "Merry Old Souls" that the famous nursery rhyme would have us believe. Indeed, many stories tell us that old kings often set impossible tasks that must be solved or challenged with tricky riddles. And woe betide the one who cannot perform the task or solve the riddle.

By bringing together all the stories in the piece, stimulated by images or words, and comparing them, children begin to see the big picture. One group of children said, "This poem is like a fairy tale, but it doesn't have a 'so they lived happily ever after' ending."

In the case studies cited, the aim of the work was to encourage inquiry on the part of the children rather than to re-create the story.

Role-playing was employed in several situations because it is such an effective way to encourage children to step into the events of books and into the lives of characters.

The imaginations of the children were stretched by encouraging them to explore incidents briefly hinted at and incidents that didn't occur but might have, and to comment on story events in the shoes of characters who were or were not present.

In so doing, the children's understanding of themes, events, and characters was amplified, and their experiences of the story broadened in a variety of ways.

## Before, during, and after the Story

'But if there is no teacher in there constantly encouraging, probing, pushing, delighting and challenging kids to read widely and deeply within and beyond their immediately perceived horizons, who will do it?'

Paul Brock,
*Teaching Literature*[12]

For teachers who grew up in an environment where the study of stories constituted a hunt for similes, metaphors, and "right answers", the dilemma of how to handle stories in the classroom can be a serious one.

Many experiences with story bring deep satisfaction and immediate response in the form of laughter, tears, or silent contemplation. It is not always productive or indeed necessary to translate these feelings into a written response or interpretive sketch. Yet how do we do our job? How do we know if we are nurturing and enabling each child's ability to interpret and appreciate?

Perhaps we should remind ourselves that as teachers, our job is to pay attention to the meanings which children bring to the story; we must open the story in an exploratory way to encourage reflective response. In so doing, we encourage children to make their viewpoints known, not just to monitor their progress in listening or reading, but to obtain an overall view of how they are seeing the fictional world in all its aspects.

Imaginations are developed by play and teachers must keep this in mind too when planning "literary journeys" with their students.

Certainly, every written story will make its own demands of us as readers, thus we must pay attention to how we approach it. For example, a short piece, sketchy in detail, may require considerable elaboration with few restrictions other than that the basic facts be adhered to. In such instances, our most detailed work with the story will take place during the reading of it as we continue to examine it in different contexts. What we are doing is broadening the perceptions of the children about the material.

A case in point might be Charles Causley's twentieth-century nursery rhyme, "Charity Chadder".

CHARITY CHADDER

Charity Chadder
Borrowed a ladder,
Leaned it against the moon,
Climbed to the top
Without a stop
On the 31st of June,
Brought down every single star,
Kept them all in a pickle jar.[13]

An initial reading of the text could involve the children in unison speaking, two choruses handling alternating lines. Extended work might involve identifying solo parts working in combination with chorus parts. Eventually, attempts might be made to work with different arrangements or styles, varying from upbeat and jazzy to lamenting and despairing.

Another close reading of the text might seek to identify the storyteller, the storyteller's intent, and the audience for the tale. Because speculation is called for, the children can feel free to wrap the lines in a wide variety of contexts. Searching for the story's voice can produce some quite exciting interpretations. Some of the voices which one class attempted included:

- the stars themselves telling of their kidnapping and weeping over their sorry plight;
- a storyteller and chorus enjoying a call-and-response improvisation of the lines;
- Charity's girlfriends celebrating yet another fearless feat of this feckless heroine;
- anchor desk and on-site reports dealing with a crisis on the six o'clock news;
- a grandparent retelling the story of Charity's afternoon picking of blossoms from a cherry tree as an extended metaphor;
- Charity herself delivering a dramatic monologue in praise of her adventure.

Now that the text has been surrounded with a set of stories, it can be reread with a view to seeking the stories inside. This is best achieved by encouraging the children to raise their own questions about the selection. One group of nine-year-olds asked the following:

- Why did she steal the stars?
- Why wasn't she caught?
- Was she wearing anything special at the time?
- Stars would be burning hot; how did she get them down?
- How long did it take?
- What did she do with the stars once they were in jars?
- Did this story take place on a mountain top?
- How did people feel about the theft?
- The stars are back now, so she must have been caught. How did this happen?
- How can the moon be protected if she strikes again?
- How did the stars get put back?

If the children are encouraged to think about their most important questions, some exciting new stories can emerge. One class wished to pursue the idea about capturing the thief, Charity. They invented amazing sky traps (how like so many ancient myths!) and a story about how Charity was captured.

Another class wished to tackle the problem of returning the

stars to their rightful place. Interestingly enough, rather than invoking the supernatural, they came up with a story that centred on human resourcefulness as a solution.

Reading beyond the story could be the next step. Throughout the world and across all cultures, human beings have told of their fearful visions of darkened skies devoid of moon and stars. A search among the world's myths could turn up dozens of stories to explain mysterious disappearances of stars or moon. Such exploration helps children to understand the interrelatedness of all the world's stories. Charles Causley's "Charity Chadder" may be an invention of the 1980s, but it is no more than a continuation of a story that has been told since human beings first began to tell each other stories.

Some stories require extensive consideration before reading in order to overcome difficulties which might get in the way of understanding or enjoyment. In one classroom, a teacher wishing to use Donald Carrick's *Harald and the Giant Knight* with his Grade 4 pupils as an introduction to a theme on knights and castles, thought it important that the children understand that one of the significant differences between life in medieval times and life today for the ordinary person centred on the opportunity to make choices. He created a situation where the children taking the roles of medieval peasants were able to discover the relationship between themselves and the landholding barons who were their landlords. In the course of this exploration, the children also made important discoveries about the societal functions of knights of the time. By the time they came to the story, the children were able to identify strongly with the plight of young Harald and his parents who were faced with severe life-threatening problems when the knights from the baron's castle took over their fields during spring planting in order to carry out their battle training.

A group of six-year-olds had listened to *Little Sister and the Month Brothers* by Beatrice Schenk de Regniers read by their teacher. At the conclusion of the story, they displayed keen interest in a magic staff owned by the Month Brothers. With this staff, the brothers could change the weather in a given location on demand. The teacher permitted the children to pursue their interest in this aspect of the story. Over the next few days, they created staffs of rolled newspaper, then painted and decorated them. In the play corner, the staffs stimulated much spontaneous play. Eventually, the children wrote collectively a book of rules for the use of magic staffs.

In the spontaneous play with the staffs, they often recreated moments from the original story. Taking note of this, the teacher developed a drama lesson, using other characters from the original story. Essentially the drama developed around the need of some characters in the story to borrow the powerful staff from the Month Brothers. In dealing with this problem, the children had a rewarding experience relating present circumstance to past memory of story characters and events. In contemplating the terrible responsibilities of owning an object so powerful, they were clarifying their understanding of human strengths and frailties.

In the following example, a class had just listened to the story of Theseus and the Minotaur. Identifying with mythic heroes and monsters is no mean feat. In order to bring the children into closer contact with the story, the teacher attempted to personalize it by bringing the story down to a level where the children could empathize with characters who were not actually central to the story but would be part of the background.

She asked the children to think about ordinary people living long ago and to work with partners to depict in movement three tasks that might take up the time of folk living then. The children quickly came up with dozens of ideas — doing laundry, chopping wood, playing games, feeding babies, and so on. They all discussed the many ideas they had conceived.

Next the children were asked to think about ordinary people living on the island of Crete during the reign of King Minos and the lifetime of the Minotaur in the Labyrinth. Once again they were to work with a partner and depict three activities. This time, half the class watched while the other half performed their movement studies. Observers were instructed to find examples of what made these scenes so different from the previous ones.

In the discussion that followed, the children indicated that they had noticed the following:

- There was much evidence of people carrying weapons while performing ordinary tasks such as harvesting, hanging up laundry, and so on.

- There was much evidence of people practising with and caring for weapons — e.g., sharpening swords.
- Many people were depicted in attitudes of prayer.
- Movements tended to be jerky and nervous.
- There was a general atmosphere of watchfulness and tension.

The teacher asked the children to sum up what they thought described the general feeling and attitude of the citizens of Crete. The children concluded: "These are people living in fear."

The teacher asked the children to take this further by creating some graffiti that might have appeared on the walls of their city. The children used felt-tipped markers on large sheets of newsprint to design their graffiti, then taped their papers along one side of the classroom. The graffiti wall was an important indication of the feelings, wishes, and fears of the villagers. For example, the following appeared:

Frank used to be here.
God kill the Minotaur.
Let us live in peace.
No more of this.
Help us!
A picture of a large red demon bore the caption, "King Minos". Another symbol was a minotaur drawn inside a circle with a solid bar across it indicating "forbidden".

The teacher, in role, entered the area close to the wall and began to examine the symbols and messages, then turned to the children and asked, "Please, I think you can help me." In the scene that followed, the teacher introduced herself as the parent of an Athenian youth destined to be sacrificed to the Minotaur. She wanted to know if there was anything that might be done to prevent the tragedy. At first the children, quickly slipping into the roles of villagers, wanted to know how someone from Athens had come ashore and wanted to determine if she were actually a traitor. Once satisfied that they could trust the stranger, they quickly referred to the events of the story to explain the present situation, then confided their own thoughts about the annual ritual. "When the Athenian youths are led from the ships to the Labyrinth I feel ashamed," said one villager. "Each spring my family and I hide in a cave when the Athenian boys and girls are brought to the Minotaur," said another. The stranger then challenged the villagers to accompany her to the palace of King Minos and let their true feelings be known. The villagers protested vigorously that such action would be futile, and would result in the deaths of all involved.

The teacher, still in role, rebuked the villagers, accusing them of being little more than animals, hiding in caves and living in misery. The villagers were stunned at this accusation, but no one ventured forth to accompany the stranger, who said, "I go now to appeal to King Minos not only for the life of my own daughter, but for your lives too."

The drama ended. The room was electric!

Although the nature of this kind of work will be discussed more later, it is important to draw attention to several of its positive outcomes. Children who had expressed little enthusiasm for the story initially became quite vocal during the activity. Children who might be characterized as weaker readers participated as fully as the others, arguing vociferously when occasion demanded it. All the children became problem posers and joined in the spirit of inquiry with considerable commitment. All the children had time to savor the story, formulate their responses to it, and make their meanings public.

It takes time to grow with a story — a lifetime. How can we persuade teachers to allow story to seep into the child's mind, to build curriculum modules that not only allow for extended time with a story, but demand that children savor and wonder about and wander among the words and ideas, the shadows of a tale?

Dorothy Heathcote describes storying as a journey that takes you into a labyrinth of inquiry, a quest in which you bump up against things you know and stumble against things you never even thought of knowing; you are "surprised into knowing." The outer form of this journey is not the learning: the struggle is the learning process, the part between the starting and the outer completion.

## CHAPTER 5

# *A Story Response Repertoire*

HOW ALL STORIES CAME AMONG MEN

Mouse goes everywhere. Through rich men's houses she creeps, visiting even the poorest. At night, with her little bright eyes, she watches the doing of secret things and no treasure chamber is so safe but she can tunnel through and see what is hidden there.

In the old days she wove four story children from all that she saw, and to each of these she gave a gown of different colors — white, red, blue, and black. The stories became her children and lived in her house and served her, because she had no children of her own.

North American Indian folktale[1]

## Modes of Responding

We described in the last chapter our reasons for helping children respond to the stories they have listened to or read. This may not be an easy task. There are many educators whom we respect who believe that directed activities after a story can not only damage the initial experience but actually destroy it. We have seen this occur and we have no doubt been responsible for similar losses. but in this book, we are concerned with the class as a group, as a community, and after an experience of story, there are many learning opportunities that must not be passed up. Safeguards lie in seeking the many modes of responding as a repertoire of choices, and in letting the children select and direct their own learning as much as possible. We may begin with a concept — set out art supplies, divide the class into discussion groups, organize an interview — but the children will make the meaning, and we as teachers will have to be sensitive to their wants and needs. Because we story together, the group of young people will have to cooperate and collaborate in carrying out activities. Not all children will be working on identical projects: some may be in groups, others may be partners, and others may work on their own for the moment.

Nonetheless — in order to refocus, to share, to demonstrate — the children will come together and learn from each other in the community setting.

We have set out eight response modes in the repertoire that teachers can use, but we admit that each mode is not discrete from the others. Role-playing will involve talk; writing may involve role-play: the story we retell may be written down. However, we trust that teachers will make use of the components of response in innovative and exciting ways, and that they will develop their own methods of organizing storying activities.

Some types of stories dictate the work that will follow: controversial endings require talk for clarification; a beautifully illustrated picture book may beg for art or media activities. Similarly, some groups of children will be hesitant to share unless a sense of trust is created; the room in which the children meet the story may necessitate specific types of work. We hope that as we describe each mode and demonstrate particular lessons in which children respond to a story, teachers will use professional judgment in determining their own response program. Our advice would be to listen to the children, listen to the story, and listen to your own teaching wisdom.

What follows is a brief overview of the eight response modes we use; each will be discussed in greater detail later in the chapter.

## A Response Repertoire

1. STORY TALK

- gossiping and commenting about stories
- discussing who we are in the story, the story events, the context, the impact, the style

- talking about other story sets, such as genres, versions, themes, styles, authors, culture, art, structure
- having presentations, seminars, debates about story issues
- interviewing the authors, those written about, those who read the story
- reporting background information
- brainstorming, problem-solving, making decisions
- establishing buzz groups, literature circles
- exploring feelings and thoughts both inside and outside the story
- generating questions and connections that arise from the story
- sharing discoveries

2. TELLING AND RETELLING STORIES

- telling our own anecdotes and stories
- retelling the story from a personal point of view
- sharing personal experiences that relate to the story
- revisiting the story in role as a witness or character
- telling stories that connect to or grow from this story
- playing storytelling games and activities growing out of the story

3. STORY DRAMA

- role-playing situations from the story, both child-initiated and teacher-initiated
- exploring ideas, events, and concepts in the story
- developing analogies to the story
- placing characters from the story in new contexts
- using the mood or atmosphere of the story in a drama
- exploring the story through movement, mime, or puppetry
- using the story as a source for scripts, as in readers' theatre

4. READING STORIES ALOUD

- sharing favorite sections with friends
- reading selected pieces in a book talk
- reading our own written responses to others

- introducing the story to others by reading a section aloud
- taping the story for a listening centre
- building a cooperative chant for choral speaking
- reading the dialogue as script
- reading the narration aloud while others move or mime
- reading to a buddy or a younger child

## 5. WRITING OUR OWN STORIES

- patterning stories from the original
- writing versions and variants of the story
- revealing feelings and ideas stimulated by the story
- writing in role from the story
- connecting information and research to the story
- developing plot diagrams and story webs
- inventing other stories inspired by this one
- writing letters to authors, characters, each other
- using journals to record thoughts and emotions

## 6. PARALLEL READING

- reading other stories by the same author, illustrator, or collector
- reading other stories connected to the theme, the concept, the style, the culture of the original
- locating background information and research
- reading about the author or illustrator
- reading non-fiction stories that relate to the story
- finding reviews and reports about the book or the author
- reading stories written by other children related to the story

## 7. STORY VISUALS

- responding to ideas and feelings through art media
- setting up displays, for instance on bulletin boards, related to the story, theme, or author
- mapping and graphing incidents in the story
- constructing three-dimensional art
- making posters, book covers, advertisements from the story
- using other media to represent the story — filmstrip, video, slides

- locating films, videos, or art reproductions relating to the story

8. CELEBRATING STORIES AND AUTHORS

- interviewing guest authors and illustrators who visit
- creating book talks on a theme or concept
- attending a young authors' conference
- setting up displays of artifacts that represent the story
- reading about authors, their views and lives
- writing and "publishing" our own books
- setting up special story celebrations for the whole school

## Story Talk

The young student teachers we work with sometimes recoil at the thought of a discussion after a child has read a book. "But won't it ruin the book for her? Won't it destroy the memories that have been built up? Won't it trivialize the understanding that has developed over the private reading time?" We appreciate the concern; such problems may have developed from traditional novel study programs that teachers have met in their latter years of schooling. But in our work, story talk is the main ingredient of learning. The children talk to learn, storying in their own words, digging inside the narrative, floating above it, looking at it through magnifying glasses as they would a rare stamp from India, examining it through telescopes like an undiscovered planet, but most important, revising and remaking their stories because of what others are thinking and revealing about their own stories.

We talk to children individually, in groups, and as a class. We used to enjoy using recess time for a private one-on-one story interview. One child would volunteer to take part in a book talk with the teacher as they patroled the playground, interrupted by an occasional remonstration by the teacher to a group who were roughhousing. But in ten to twelve minutes, much could be said about the child's response to the story he or she had read. Often the child would raise the questions or points to be explored. Sometimes we would have prepared two or three issues that we felt would help in the discussion. But usually, as the talk flowed, the ideas to be worked on seemed to come up in a natural manner. There was something about the outdoors and the noise and the intimacy that promoted a particular freedom of thought. We value those times.

Classroom conferencing can take place in ten seconds or half an hour, depending upon the situation. Often a special corner or seating place can encourage a child to open up concerns. The teacher may want to give the child some lead-in activity as preparation for the conference. The child may request an interview during the reading of the story for help with story background or concept development. The teacher may want to interview the child before a book is read, relating other books to the new one, informing and explaining the background, the author, the time, the place. Story concerns may be shared in one-on-one conferences that are private and personal, and may only arise in this type of trusted relationship. Story can trigger very powerful responses in children, and good teachers can seize the opportunity to place perspective and compassion in the response frame.

Story talk in a small group offers a powerful dynamic for learning. The discussion can be spontaneous or directed. The children can put forward their own concerns or work from a stimulus-response sheet. They can meet together before reading to predict, anticipate, and set the stage for the narrative. They can use story talk as the starting point for story projects of all kinds — research, role-playing, writing, storytelling, reading aloud, painting. By beginning with story talk, the teacher allows all the areas of comprehension concerns to be brought into the open, so that children can begin making meaning, both personal and collective, using the medium of talk — invisible print that can be edited and reformed so easily — to understand the depth of the printed or spoken story. The teacher may work with one group at a time, as moderator or contributor, or a student reader may volunteer or be selected. Some talk can be tape-recorded for playback as clarification or for another group to hear. Story talk with the whole class is an effective use of the talk mode, but it presents some difficulties. The number of children who can respond during the session is limited by time, opportunity, the ability of each child to speak aloud in large groups, and the group's ability to listen and respond sensitively and meaningfully. It may be difficult to hear unless the furniture is rearranged. Whole class story talk may be best used for:

- brainstorming ideas about concerns for discussion in small groups;
- predicting and anticipating and clarifying the story to be read or heard;
- relating the story to other classroom concerns, such as thematic units, genre, or style;
- building background about the story's setting, characters, concept structure;
- allowing a forum for summarizing, bringing forth points of view;
- sharing talk that happened during group interaction;
- allowing for feedback and different interpretations;
- giving opportunities for film and video versions of story, and for authors and illustrators to lecture and demonstrate;
- setting up occasions for panels, seminars, public speakers, interviews, debates.

Story talk with the whole class presents a public forum for shared common experiences related to story. It allows for reflective talk after other response modes have been explored. Children can talk about the pictorial representations, the writing, the drama, the research, etc. The talk may focus on the story meanings or on the storyteller, on the children's identification with the story, on the stories within the story, on the background information, on the conflict, the resolution, the use of language, the difficulty of idiom, the word choice, the sentence structure, the style. It is important that the story talk at times be focused on the story itself, whether at the beginning of story talk, or as a summary or reflection of the dialogue that has taken place. The children may leave the story in order to understand it better, but they should return to see its reflection in the new learning, the new meaning that has grown from the talk.

We were asked to address two Grade 6 classes and their parents in a rural Canadian community for their graduation ceremony. We chose to read Katherine Paterson's book *The Crane Wife*, a beautiful reworking of an old Japanese folktale. It is a story of a poor man who saves the life of a wounded crane, and later is rewarded when he marries a young woman. Their happiness wanes as their poverty grows, and she offers to weave for him cloth to sell at market, on the condition that he does not watch her as she works. He agrees, and the beautiful cloth is sold for a handsome amount of money. Of course, the husband requests that she once again weave the cloth, and she consents. Upon his neighbors' urging, he orders her a third time to work her magic, but this time he slides the door open and sees a crane ripping out her feathers in order to weave. She sees him, and flies away, never to return. For us, it is a tale of trust and honor, and we felt it suitable for young people about to enter junior high school.

We asked the children for their comments after we had read the story, their feelings about the man or the crane wife, and one girl asked, "How do you weave cloth?" We briefly described the process and attempted to refocus the discussion, but other students interrupted our progress with other questions and concerns about the making of cloth, and we realized that for these children at this time, "The Crane Wife" is the story of weaving. We asked them to look at the labels in their shirts and sweaters for the place of origin of the cloth, and then listed all the countries they found on the blackboard. After calling out over forty locales, the class asked why Canada wasn't represented on any of the labels. This caused them to search further — their pants, skirts, even underwear. We noticed that the parents were joining in the quest, and in fact, everyone was looking at each other's clothes for the honor of their country. At last, a small voice cried out, "In my running shoe, I found it: 'Made in Canada'!" All the people, young and old, applauded with a standing ovation as the two of us left the room.

The children had directed the journey; we were only guides along the route. We had begun with a theme that held little interest for the children, and we were forced to abandon it during the session. In a regular classroom setting, we could perhaps bring the talk around to why, in Japanese folklore, weaving held such a prominent place, or why the supernatural character was the one who spun cloth, but the children should decide how to begin the story talk, and their contributions should help us develop the learning areas.

To encourage story talk, the teacher asks questions. The art of teaching lies in those questions and in handling the responses they engender. If we list our questions, we should be influenced by the children's questions as well, and therefore our personal list must never be seen as sequential or controling or a dull list to be covered. They are signposts for the journey, and may be welcomed as directions when the talk becomes disjointed or argumentative.

Perhaps the most important question to be considered is, "Tell me about the story." This can begin the journey inside. The teacher must create a middle ground that allows the children to learn about the story, balancing the response among their experiences of the story — thoughts, feelings, and observations during and after the story — with the content of the story itself — theme, plot, characters, and form.

In *Booktalk*, Aidan Chambers has provided a very useful chapter dealing with sample questions of an open-ended nature which have helped to provide lively interchanges of personal meanings among youngsters.[2] Although a long list of sample questions has been provided, Chambers once stated in a workshop that the following four questions would stimulate all the discussion you could hope to have.

1. Tell me about the parts you liked most.
2. Tell me about the parts you didn't like.
3. Was there anything that puzzled you?
4. Did you notice anything in the story/poem that made a pattern?

A librarian had just completed a unit on dinosaurs, and the children from Kindergarten to Grade 6 had gathered in the library to celebrate the unit. We were asked to speak to them and share in the completion of their work, and we brought with us seven or eight books related to dinosaurs. However, the children had experienced all our books but one, *What Happened to Patrick's Dinosaurs?* by Carol Carrick, with pictures by Donald Carrick, a sequel to *Patrick's Dinosaurs*, which they knew. We read the book aloud and presented the illustrations to the audience. Once again, Patrick is defending his love of dinosaurs to his big brother Hank, and describes how the dinosaurs were friendly to people, building them a modern world, until the unhappy dinosaurs left the earth and civilization took a backward step. When we, tongue-in-cheek, agreed with Patrick's theory, the children reacted violently with all kinds of arguments and theories as to why dinosaurs and humans had not co-existed. Their information was surprising, and it was articulated well. Only the five-year-olds remained on our side in the discussion. At the end of the period, we were in disgrace with a victorious audience, until we brought out our last book, a rallying cry for Patrick, called *We're Back*!

Teachers often ask us where the ideas come from for story talk, but we have no single answer: the children, you, your parents, the street outside, the picture on the cover of a book, the name of the author, the color of the jacket, the memories that flood from the story, the people like you in the story or those totally different, the tears of the boy in the back row, the laughter of the girl in the front, the rhythm of the words, the taste of them as you speak them, the newspaper at breakfast, the label on your shirt, the vibrations of the class, the rainbow in the sky. We tune in to the story with the children and together we make meaning through story talk.

## Telling and Retelling Stories

### USING OUR OWN WORDS

Retelling a story in one's own words is one of the most effective ways to achieve a reflective response. Fortunately, this is an activity that can be organized simply.

So often reading and the activities around reading are "hurry up, hurry up" — we are getting through the text, through the story, through the book, through the course, through the whatever. You miss so much if you don't have a chance to linger with a story. But by encouraging children to retell a story, you can enable them to go back to that story and find out more and more.

One of the things we like to do with children is round robin storytelling (not to be confused with round robin reading, which is now taboo). One after the other, in a circle, we simply retell a story we have heard or read, in our own words, with the idea that it is the responsibility of the whole group to tell the story. Each of us only has a part of it for a few seconds before we pass it on. Using that as a device we have been able to get children thinking about point of view, and telling stories in the first person, third person, or mixing up a first-person narration with a third-person narration, two first-person speakers, and all of these in combination. These produce interesting storytelling and the more we do that, the more the children begin to project themselves imaginatively into the text.

As the story is told, we begin to see a very rich new story appearing. In the context of that new story, we will very often ask the children their feelings and thoughts about the characters. We then come out of the circle and do interviews with each other. "Let's interview this person. Pretend you are a reporter. What would you like to ask? What would you like to know?" That simple technique gets the children talking about the characters. Next, we might have the whole bunch altogether, all telling stories at once, or we might have a surprise interview with a character, with only three questions, just like the three wishes so common in folktales. Then we get them to refine their understanding of what they think is important about the story, arguing and struggling with the three questions that are going to give them the inside information. After that we go back into our storytelling circles and tell the story one more time, only now we must reveal a big secret that we discovered about the story that nobody else knows.

We have sometimes recorded these little story circles and listened to the tapes. Often what started out as a very narrow, tiny little segment of a story has grown and become very rich. We go back and examine other questions. How did the author tell this story? How did we tell this story? At this point we are so inside the story we're getting into everything from character development to dialogue to structure, without ever using any of those words. The storytelling way offers hands-on experience.

Spontaneous retelling in a story circle is one of the most effective ways that children can reveal what a story they have just heard has meant to them. With such retelling, no one has the burden of the entire story. As the story travels around the circle, each participant can add as much or as little as desired. Indeed, some children often prefer to pass on the initial round or so until they begin to get more involved in the story. The beauty of this activity is its simplicity and the opportunity it affords each child to put the story into his or her own words and to make explicit personal story imagery. It is also an extremely effective way to hone listening skills.

The same kind of story retelling also works effectively in pairs.

In this instance, the story alternates back and forth, perhaps at a signal by the teacher. Initially, it helps to keep signaling a change every twenty to thirty seconds until the children feel confident that they can make more extended runs. Small groups can function in like fashion once the children have become accustomed to working with stories this way. Sometimes it's good to have members of a group act out a story as one of its members tells it. Again, the emphasis is on spontaneous retelling. Once under way, the listeners add actions, sound effects, choruses, whatever comes into their heads. Such activity often serves to free up a story and to make the children more aware of the possibilities that exist for retelling that story. In one such exercise, a class developed, through their play with the material, the following innovations:

- a chorus chant;
- animation of inanimate objects;
- use of considerable dialogue;
- elaboration on the story characters which gave them a greater complexity;
- less exposition and greater immediacy.

Another form of large-group, spontaneous retelling might be called communal composition. It involves composing orally together from a subject or theme. In some ways, it resembles rapping. The object of the activity is to improvise with words, rhythms, and sounds using a single theme or subject.

The theme or subject is discussed in terms of what information the group has about it. This material is sorted, classified, and ordered into an "out-loud" experience. For example, a composition on how words play might result in an inventory of all the ways this occurs (e.g., palindromes, puns, etc.) and examples of these in action. A framework of unison choruses, antiphonal choruses, solos, and songs are then developed.

One teacher capitalized on her classes' interest in proverbs. She introduced to her children John Agard's *Say It Again, Granny*, a collection of twenty poems based on Caribbean proverbs. It became the source for the following group composition.

| | |
|---|---|
| All: | Granny says (chanted three times with sharp rhythmic clapping "dada-da-dada" interspersed between the words). |
| Group A (unison): | Early to bed and early to rise<br>Makes one healthy, wealthy, and wise. |
| Group B (unison): | That's what Granny says! |
| Group B (unison): | Birds of a feather flock together. |
| Group A (unison): | That's what Granny says! |
| Group B (unison): | Mother, may I go out to swim? |
| Group B (unison): | Yes, darling granddaughter.<br>Hang your clothes on a hickory stick<br>But don't go near the water. |
| Group B (unison chanting under solos): | Granny always telling you |
| Solo A | A stitch in time saves nine, |
| Solo B | Don't count your chickens before they hatch, |
| Solo C | Still waters run deep. |

The end of the piece was played as a game. The children were divided into groups and given a proverb to disguise by "padding" it. For example, the proverb, "A watched pot never boils", might become, "A vessel containing $H_2O$ seldom reaches 100°C. when scrutinized constantly."

Each group in turn chanted its "padded proverb", while the rest of the class tried to echo the original one.

While much of the preceding may not seem to be storytelling, it is important to point out that language creativity or word play reinforces the fact that words have sounds, rhythms, spellings, and visual shapes — all qualities that can be played with and that contribute to the power of language which makes a story live.

Prepared retellings differ from the spontaneous mainly in that the children work from print sources rather than spoken ones. The emphasis is still on having them use their own words, which can be tricky because where print is involved, the children often think that everything that is written down must be reproduced exactly.

Working from print sources can involve techniques like the following:

1. The entire class is divided into groups of no more than three members.

2. Each group is given a piece of a story to retell as a trio. How the group retells it is entirely up to them; the only rule is that each member of the group must be involved in telling.

3. The groups reconvene and form a story circle. The group with the opening segment begins. The remaining groups have to figure out where their segment fits and come in at the appropriate time.

This technique works particularly well when formula tales are used as source material. The patterns and repetition help the tellers to anticipate and predict, thus exposing the class to some of the tricks of the trade of the oral tradition.

Storytelling of this nature can also provide opportunities to visit "story families" in ways that familiarize children with important collections that they might not otherwise discover. For example, the "Jataka Tales", although little known in America, have been told for over two thousand years in other parts of the world. Attributed to Buddha, they are to eastern cultures what Aesop's fables are to the west. The stories feature animals that speak and act much as humans do. They are, in fact, a wonderful introduction to other animal stories of enchantment which children might encounter, such as *The Tale of Peter Rabbit* (Beatrix Potter), *The Jungle Book* (Rudyard Kipling), *Charlotte's Web* (E. B. White), *Abel's Island* (William Steig), *The Sheep Pig* (Dick King Smith), *Watership Down* (Richard Adams), and *Ratha's Creature* (Clare Bell).

This is also an interesting way to explore genres. The "tall tale" or the "trickster tale" could become the focus of work which, if approached imaginatively, could span the globe, inviting wonderful comparisons. Think of *Doctor Coyote* by John Bierhorst, Aesop's fables carried to South America, taken over by the Inca, and incorporated into their Coyote Trickster Stories.

Prepared retellings can also involve completely changing the form of a story. One group of children used Leon Garfield's unique retelling of the story of the tower of Babel (*Nimrod's Tower*) as the source for their invention.

They proceeded by isolating key moments in the story and rewriting them as playground songs, skipping rhymes, and ball-bouncing chants.

Here are some of the pieces they composed:

1. *The Story of the Labourers*

Fetch and carry
Fetch and carry
Nimrod the King is building a tower
It's to be as high as Heaven,
A spot's been chosen
The clay's been dug
There's brick and stone for us to hold
And ten thousand labourers to do as they are
told . . .
Lift
Heave
Push

2. *The Chant of the Foreman*

Stay at work! Stay at work! says foreman to workers
Stay at work! Stay at work! says foreman to workers
Stay at work! Stay at work! says foreman to workers
You've got to build higher or we'll stop your pay
Heave bricks and mortar, says foreman to workers
(repeat twice)
You must pass through clouds or we'll stop your pay.
Higher and higher, says foreman to workers
(repeat twice)
You must reach for eagles or we'll stop your pay.

3. *The Chant of the Stonemasons*

This is the stone
   That was hauled on the backs
      Of workers who were ordered
         By loud-shouting foremen
            To "Hurry along there,
               And build a great tower
                  For Nimrod the King
                     Who would challenge the Lord."

### 4. *The Cry of the Spectators*

Old King Nimrod climbed his tower
Old King Nimrod stayed an hour
Old King Nimrod challenged the Lord
Old King Nimrod was quickly floored.

Once they had assembled their pieces, the children formed groups and each group worked with one piece. The work involved speaking the words aloud and inventing a game that might accompany the words. Balls, ropes, and hoops were available to be incorporated into the games.

When all the games were invented and the accompanying rhymes integrated with the action patterns, the children established a plan for retelling.

They decided to create a busy playground scene alive with sound and movement.

The story was played out in a gymnasium. The children cleared the space. Then, on the signal of a bell, they streamed into the playing area, set up their games, and commenced the stories. On prearranged whistle signals, everyone froze action while each group, in agreed-upon order, did its part.

A ringing school bell ended the action and the children cleared the floor as in the beginning.

Aidan Chambers says that having older children share stories with students in younger grades is a wonderful way to bring about critical understanding because it is always easier to discuss literature that you have outgrown, that belongs to your past — work that is probably new to your audience, or just beyond their capacity as readers. All good critical discussion and writing comes from familiarity with a story and from having grown beyond the experience of it.

No one can push a child into understanding symbolism and abstraction beyond his or her current abilities. Children must be allowed to respond on their own terms, refine their ideas by being exposed to story and to the complexities of shared responses. As the teacher organizes response activities, both the children and the teacher can learn and grow from story misunderstandings, from complexities that were unclear to the children, from new-found evidence or experiences from the new learning that is generated by each retelling, by each shared response discovery. The role of the teacher is to promote further exploration of the story ideas, so that the children can help each other to broaden and deepen understandings.

The stories which our students make and tell about themselves should be honored in our classrooms, for it is through their stories that they build their self-esteem and sense of belonging in the world.

At first, children may not think they have any stories to tell, but existing stories will help them think of new stories of their own.

What's your name?
Pudd'n Tame. Ask me again
And I'll tell you the same!

Anonymous

Names or nicknames are the subject of hundreds of poems and stories. They are excellent triggers for helping children to tell the stories associated with their own names. Who were you named after? Do you know the meaning of your name? How did you get your nickname? Would you change your name?

Once children feel at ease telling "true" stories about their names, families, etc., homes and neighborhoods can be mined for tall tales, jokes, superstitions, recipes, remedies, proverbs, riddles, and much more. All this can lead to talking, writing, and storytelling of every conceivable description.

Books such as the following can stimulate children to find better ways to shape and relate their personal stories:

*The Chalk Doll*, by Charlotte Pomerantz
Rose has a cold and she wants her mother to tell her stories. The stories she wants are about her mother's childhood in Jamaica. She has heard these stories before and at times adds to the simple home narratives the important details that are etched in her mind.

*Granny Was a Buffer Girl*, by Berlie Doherty
A young woman prepares to leave home for a year's study. She

128

has not been separated from her family before. The family stories told on the eve of her departure serve to bring her to a closer understanding of her past and her culture.

*Great-Grandfather, the Baby and Me*, by Howard Knotts
A little boy tearfully awaits the return from hospital of his parents with a new baby sister. Sensing the boy's distress, his great-grandfather tells him a story of loneliness out on the Canadian prairies, and of the importance of riding miles to visit a new baby.

*Mabel's Story*, by Jenny Koralek
Grandfather turns the tables on Mabel and asks her for a bedtime story. She obliges with a tale that conjures up images of Hans Christian Andersen. Grandfather is as much a superstar listener as Mabel is a superstar narrator.

*My Name Is Emily*, by Morse and Emily Hamilton
The role of story and fantasy play in dealing with the consequences of our actions is the subject of this gentle, heartwarming confrontation between a father and his five-year-old runaway daughter.

*Say It Again, Granny*! by John Agard
Caribbean proverbs are the subject of the twenty poems in this collection. An excellent catalyst for local proverb collecting and possible reworking into other forms.

*Tales of a Gambling Grandma*, by Dayal Kaur Khalsa
Remembered incidents of her grandmother's life are the subject of the storyteller's tale. The incidents range from hilarious to sobering and point to the role that fantasy plays in the reconstruction of true-life experience. What makes the book so wonderful is its chronicling of a very special relationship between a grandmother and a child and the role of stories in bringing them together.

"William's Version", in *Nothing to Be Afraid of*, by Jan Mark
A precocious pre-schooler wants a story from his granny but can't tolerate her deviations from the tale as he sees it. The talk in

and around the story reveals a lot about William's emotional state as he contemplates the arrival of a new baby in his life.

Everyone has a neighborhood story about the house you don't visit on Hallowe'en or the strange neighbor who strikes terror into your heart whenever your ball accidentally ends up on his or her lawn. Perhaps there is a special tree or a particular animal that is the subject of much neighborhood chat. A mystery, a special happening, a tree downed in a storm, an annual bed race — every neighborhood has stories.

One book that might stir some neighborhood story making is *The Green Lion of Zion Street* by Julia Fields. In this lively narrative poem, a group of school children, bored with waiting for the school bus, embark on a foggy morning adventure across a high bridge to the spot where a stone lion prowls. As they approach it, they let their imaginations run wild and end up not only frightening themselves, but missing the bus as well. What child hasn't let a shadow, a statue, a gnarled tree, a laneway, or a creaking door become the object of a wild fantasy?

Cynthia Rylant's book *When I Was Young in the Mountains* is so carefully told that listeners young and old are ready to share their own stories of porch swings, corner stores, grandma's kitchen, swimming with snakes in the water, baptisms where the candidate is immersed completely. When they hear "for I was in the mountains, and that was always enough," storyers conjure up their own special places from childhood and from today, placing their own personal narrative alongside those of Cynthia Rylant.[3]

A walk together around the school neighborhood should furnish clues for dozens of neighborhood tales — a hole in the ground, a dark grotto, a cryptic message scribbled on a wall.

THE WORDS OF OTHERS

Probably one of the most common ways that we all tell stories using the words of others is the folk wisdom that manifests itself in the tossed-off proverbs, incantations ("Rain, rain, go away" or "A stitch in time"), and prophecies ("A sunshiney shower won't last half an hour") that lace our everyday speech.

Children come quickly to this kind of storytelling in their play in street and schoolyard. Possibly, in school they will be taught other stories in the context of singing and dramatic games — ''The Farmer in the Dell''; ''London Bridge''; ''Brown Girl''; ''The Grand Old Duke of York'', just to name a few.

In addition to the chiming in, call-and-response, and vocal play featured in such enactments, there are often simple movement patterns such as circling, advancing and retreating, passing under arches, and scattering.

STROKEYBACK

**In this game there need to be at least four players. One of them is chosen to turn her back to the others, and usually leans against a wall or lamp-post, with her face buried in her arm. The others gather round, and the leader chants:**

> North, South, East, West
> Who's the king of the crow's nest;
> Draw a snake right down her back;
> Who's the one to finish that?

When the leader has drawn the snake (by trailing a finger down the player's back), another player (taking a hint from the leader) stretches forward and pokes the first player's back. The person whose back has been poked then turns around and guesses who picked her, but — here lies the sport — she is not told whether her guess is correct. She has first to set a task for the person she has named; and it is only after she has done so that she learns whether or not her guess was correct. If it was, the person who drew the snake has to perform the task she has been set; but if the guess was wrong, the guesser herself has to carry out her own instructions.

Nursery rhymes are another common source of stories we tell using the words of others. The variety of themes, subject matter, styles, speaking voices, and genres in these rhymes is extremely valuable in helping children to click into the immediacy of these splendid short tales:

Mother, mother
I feel sick
Send for the doctor
Quick, quick, quick

In marble walls as white as milk,
Lined with a skin as soft as silk,
Within a fountain crystal clear
A golden apple doth appear.
No doors there are to this stronghold,
Yet thieves break in and steal the gold.

From these early forms of storytelling, it is but a hop, step, and jump to ballads, monologues, dialogues, song sermons, and a host of exciting narrative poems which can be spoken aloud together and which will inevitably slip into the remembered repertoire of some eager children.

THE HUNTSMAN

Kagwa hunted the lion,
Through bush and forest went his spear
One day he found the skull of a man
And said to it, "How did you come here?
The skull opened its mouth and said,
"Talking brought me here."

Kagwa hurried home;
Went to the king's chair and spoke:
"In the forest I found a talking skull."
The king was silent. Then he said slowly,
"Never since I was born of my mother
Have I seen or heard of a skull which spoke."

The king called out to his guard:
"Two of you now go with him
And find this talking skull;
But if his tale is a lie
And the skull speaks no word,
This Kagwa himself must die."

They rode into the forest;
For days and nights they found nothing.
At last they saw the skull; Kagwa

Said to it, "How did you come here?"
The skull said nothing. Kagwa implored,
But the skull said nothing.

The guards said, "Kneel down."
They killed him with sword and spear.
Then the skull opened its mouth;
"Huntsman, how did you come here?"
And the dead man answered,
"Talking brought me here."

Edward Lowbury[4]

This story poem provides an excellent source for retelling, for dramatizing the narrative and the dialogue.

## Story Drama

For a language conference, we were asked to run a demonstration lesson on creative thinking growing from story, and for our own interest we selected a poem that might appear difficult for the Grade 1 class that we were going to work with. However, one of us would read the poem to them as the voice of the story-teller inside the story poem, and the other would be the teacher building the drama with the children. The poem is one of atmosphere and feeling, and contains much subtext for exploration.

OUR POND

The pond in our garden
Is murky and deep
And lots of things live there
That slither and creep.

Like diving bell spiders
And great ramshorn snails
And whirligig beetles
And black snappertails.

There used to be goldfish
That nibbled my thumb,
But now there's just algae
And sour, crusty scum.

There used to be pondweed
With fizzy green shoots,
But now there are leeches
And horrible newts.

One day when my football
Rolled in by mistake
I tried to retrieve it
By using a rake.

But as I leaned over
A shape from the ooze
Bulged up like a nightmare
And lunged at my shoes.

I ran back in shouting,
But everyone laughed
And said I was teasing
Or else I was daft.

But I know what happened
And when I'm asleep
I dream of those creatures
That slither and creep

The diving bell spiders
And great ramshorn snails
And whirligig beetles
And black snappertails.

Richard Edwards[5]

It was interesting to see that the children at first were certain
that the character who had read the poem had seen nothing in
reality in the pond. They mentioned that he perhaps had had
a daydream or that he was prone to exaggeration. However, the
character's belief in the creature prompted one child to explain
that perhaps it had been a shadow. When asked what might have
caused that shadow the children offered many suggestions, the
most interesting of which was Tanya's description of a bird house
in the next yard looking like a thing on the surface of the pond,
and when a bird left the pond, the shadow seemed to move
inside the water.

Then the storyteller, still in role, asked one child if he wanted
to see the pool with him, and the child agreed and the two went,

hand in hand, to a corner of the room. On their return, the child announced to the others: "I saw the thing in the pool." He was of course questioned by the children, and the mystery and the drama began to deepen. Most children expressed the view that the creature existed only in the storyteller's imagination, but others volunteered to examine the pool for themselves. Two or three children accompanied the storyteller to the pool each time, and on their return explained that they too had seen the creature. When asked to describe it, they used words like "shadowy," "oozing," "dark," "slithery". In role the storyteller was very calm and very certain that he had seen the creature, and those children who had gone with him to the pool assured us that they had as well.

The teacher questioned the storyteller and the others about their ideas, and stated his doubts about anyone having seen anything. He pressed the children who had not gone to question those who had, and he interrogated those who had gone about their experience.

Near the end of the lesson, the teacher asked the storyteller to retell the experience of the pond, and the latter read the poem once more. Only one child remained who felt that the storyteller had seen nothing but shadows.

It was a fascinating experience to watch these six-year-olds gradually wander inside this complex story poem through role-playing. We use the term "story drama" to characterize this exploration of the essence of a story through improvised action.

As we noted earlier, in planning our lesson, we decided that one of us would share the poem, and the other would guide the children, but we were not sure how the process would actually work until the children began to respond. As we listened, we could sense the direction the journey would take, and we began a process of following and leading — a negotiation in role and out of role — what was developing as the children talked about their reactions to this strange story of the pond.

Making sense of a story demands that the students apply their own experiences to those in the story. The teacher must constantly help the children go back and forth between their own stories and their own responses, translating the experiences of the story into the context of their own lives. Drama, then, allows the children's own subjective worlds to come into play, helping

135

them understand the meanings of the story as they live through the drama experience. In story drama, students are required to create personal responses of their own to the story stimulus.

By joining story and drama, children can combine an interest in the lives of story characters with an inner exploration of themselves and their own struggles for control over their lives. They can become involved in role-playing, decision-making, problem-solving, verbal interaction, mime, movement, and group process, and as they do so they will develop an understanding and an appreciation of the universality of story.

The teacher can use the story to provide the stimulus for drama, and the story can assist the teacher in giving form to that drama. The story and its strength enable the teacher to dip into the richness of the contexts that the author has provided. Drama becomes a tool for the exploration of the ideas, relationships, and language of the story. The children are not limited to the facts or words in the story, since the story *per se* is not the prime focus. It may indeed happen that the children's appreciation and understanding of the story deepens after drama. However, the teacher must be concerned primarily with the developmental aspects of drama that occur as the children elaborate, extend, and invent. Story provides the framework for building drama, enriching the quality of the dramatic experience and imparting an artistic awareness to the lives of those involved.

As students begin to explore the subtext of the story, they move from an enactment of the literal information into an exploration of the concepts that lie under the plot skeleton. They begin to draw upon their own experiences and to see story incidents from the viewpoint of both self and others, entwined in a role in the drama happening at that very moment. Perhaps the children are engaged in creating a new story based on a long-ago past they never knew; perhaps they are using stereotyped memories of television adventure shows as the jumping-off point for their learning. They may feel they are simply enacting a literal story, but they will in fact be operating in an aesthetic frame of their own making.

Story drama can happen in the following situations:

1. Before students read or listen to the story, the teacher explores with the children the themes and issues abstracted

from the story or uses parallel situations from the story with other types of characters using role-playing and improvisation.

2. During the reading of the story, the teacher stops at a point where there's a problem to be solved or a decision to be made. The resulting drama activities may resolve the problems basic to the story.

3. After students have read the story, the teacher can use dramatic activity to:
   a) elaborate upon the information in the story;
   b) extend the story back in time or forward into the imagined future;
   c) invent their own story drama from the implications that they see in the story for their own lives.

4. A slight reference in a story can provide material for a drama that the children create themselves.

5. The children may be interested in particular characters in a story, and use role-playing and verbal interaction to explore motivations and relationships.

6. The teacher can add characters not found in the story and expand minor characters so that they become central to the action of the story. (Through character addition and expansion, the teacher can change the outcome of the story drama.)

7. The teacher can present an additional problem related to the story or alter the events to see what might happen.

8. The children can extend and enrich the story with ideas of their own.

The children don't have to act out the whole story or remember a script. Drama may occupy only a few minutes of the teaching schedule and can complement other teaching methods to emphasize particular aspects of the story. Drama can explore the story at one remove, through an analogy that unlocks internal comprehension. Because of the brain's ability to use metaphor, it can use the pattern of one set of images to organize quite a different set. Therefore, the images from one story can be used as images for related and yet different meanings. Story drama opens the door to an endless number of linkages in the curriculum.

The teacher is primarily a questioner who awakens the children to what they wonder about the story. Questions should be designed to focus children's knowledge of the story on new areas. The teacher must free the class from story line (plot) and involve them in the roots or concepts of the story.

> The teacher must search for a possible starting point that is relevant to the children's experience, relevant to the spirit of the story, and a vehicle for confrontation through language.
>
> Connie and Harold Rosen[6]

Occasionally a story will pose questions that might be employed to elicit spontaneous responses from listeners. A witch in a story might be interrogating passers-by about the whereabouts of a certain character or object. The storyteller, in role as the witch, might turn to a listener seated nearby and simply say something like, "Hawk, have you seen my sister's brooch?"

Usually the listener will reply. Once a group has become accustomed to this set-up, responses gradually become easier and lead to interesting elaboration of the story. It is even possible that some spontaneous conversations will become part of the tale.

Formal roles offer another kind of opportunity for involvement. A character in a story might make a comment again and again in the course of events — e.g., "If I don't hang on to some of my eggs there won't be any more chicks. Without any more chicks there won't be any more eggs!" Once listeners understand when and where this bit recurs, soloists can be invited to handle the part.

Cecily O'Neill, an authority on drama in education, writes about a classroom teacher she knows who took hold of drama and story and gave her children a powerful new tool for both making meaning collaboratively and bringing meaning to a complex picture book. Note that the drama here results not in a formal theatrical production, but in a variety of activities.

Sylvia is excited by the possibility of using drama across the curriculum. She is interested in exploring ways in which drama can illuminate and enrich her broader purposes as a teacher. One of her continuing concerns is finding ways to improve her students' reading skills. Using a favourite book — *Where the Wild Things Are* — she devised a simple but most effective drama framework to address these essential teacher concerns.

Working in role as "Max", who is now an adult, she told the class that she was very concerned about the Wild Things. For years, since Max's first visit to the Wild Things, he had been writing them letters, postcards and Christmas cards, but without ever receiving a reply. At last, he had sailed to see them once again. When he reached the island, he could see from a distance the Wild Things sitting dejectedly in a circle. In the middle of the circle was a huge heap of all the letters and cards he had written them. Suddenly, Max realised the truth. The Wild Things could not read. Now Max had come to the children to ask their help with this problem. Grown-ups were no use, since they couldn't see the Wild Things. Would they teach the creatures to read?

The children eagerly accepted the challenge. Much time was spent finding out where the Wild Things lived, and planning how to travel there and transport the creatures back to the classroom. Mapping, designing, problem-solving and decision-making were all part of this phase of the work. The children took great pains to prepare the classroom to receive the Wild Things. They considered the kind of environment which would be comfortable for the creatures. The classroom was transformed to look as much like a jungle as possible, and everything was labelled by the children to assist the Wild Things with beginning reading skills. The children made large paper Wild Things, and Sylvia paired the students so that they could support each other in their reading. The children were able to call upon her in the role as "Max" to resource and assist them in their teaching task. The children made Big Books for the creatures, and prepared other reading materials which they hoped would appeal to them. They found clever ways of pretending that their Wild Things did work which they actually did themselves. The

Wild Things wrote several books, and some read them aloud to the class in squeaky voices. Each child kept a Project Record Book for their Wild Thing, in which the creatures wrote about what they did each day. Lessons in classroom behaviour, morality, and even appropriate cuisine for the Wild Things arose as the work progressed. At one point, Sylvia invited the Reading Consultant for the area to come and work with the children in order to reinforce their instructional strategies.

At the beginning of this unit, Sylvia had asked the children to list the strategies they used to help themselves read. At the end of the work she did the same, and the children's list of strategies was more extensive, much more creative and clearly demonstrated an understanding of the reading/writing connection. They had acquired a considerable number of new strategies to improve their own reading skills. It seems clear that the children's experience as "teachers" in the drama reinforced their sense of themselves as learners: it brought the process of learning to read into explicit focus, but the activity remained one in which they possessed both status and competence. They actively promoted their own learning as well as that of the imaginary Wild things, and both inside and outside the drama they grew in skills and confidence.[7]


## Reading Stories Aloud

Traditionally, in a reading lesson, children have read stories aloud in order to check pronunciation and syntactic comprehension. Often, the oral reading preceded discussion or the written answering of comprehension questions — testing questions. However, the skills embedded in oral interpretation are complex, to say the least, and for many children, oral reading has not led to deeper or stronger interpretation of the print, but to word-calling and to correcting the pronunciation of others in the group. The repeated reading aloud of a story as a rote exercise may even decrease a child's understanding of the meaning and appreciation of the story and the words. For these and other reasons reading aloud by children has been abandoned by some dedicated teachers in the cause of student-centred teaching, and yet oral interpretation, when done well, can improve all the skills of comprehension, lead to revelation for the reader, and strengthen the grasp of a particular interpretation on the part of the listener.

Without opportunity to interrogate the story, to rub up against it, to notice how others are feeling and wondering, to question private believes, to expand information and to hear the voices of print struggling for freedom, the child will be sharing print aloud for no learning reason. A few children can decode phonetically and comprehend almost nothing. Even these, especially these, need occasion for coming to grips with the meat of the story before attempting to share their knowledge. The teller and the told are each precious in this process of reading aloud. Sometimes, it is the reader who is also listening, learning through the ear and the eye at the same time.

What models are there for reading aloud?

- A parent who has read alongside the child throughout his or her life;
- a teacher who shares what she is reading, both lines and excerpts, at the close of silent reading time;
- a teacher who delights in reading fine stories to children each and every day;
- a teacher who tells stories to the class, owning them, making them personal for the listener;
- a teacher who sings with the children, letting the story tunes fill their ears;
- a teacher who encourages oral reading only when there is an audience who wants to listen.

Can we as teachers give children the strengths required for oral reading, so that they will approach the process with interest and excitement, accepting the challenge of bringing someone else's words to life, and the risk of discovering a means of communicating learning? Perhaps this is the most complicated and sophisticated of all response modes. Teachers need to re-examine their motives and strategies for including or excluding oral reading in the language programs of their classes.

If children have access to models of oral reading, they will want to participate. The teacher can encourage them in many ways.

1. They can join in by reading songs, verses, and poems aloud.

2. They can be part of the choral speaking of poems and rhythmic stories, safely hidden from the critical ears of those who might hinder the process.

3. They can read big book stories, or favorite lines from selections on overhead transparencies and chart paper.

4. They can read their own writings aloud in small groups only after editing their print to permit ease in reading.

5. They can work with a buddy from an older class, someone who will offer an experienced shoulder to lean on as they read to each other, and delve deeply into the context of the story as they find ways to bring it to life.

6. They can read the dialogue of a story in groups as if it were from a script. The narrator will give them clues as to how to interpret the words. They can share excerpts from story novels with others who have not read the materials, so that the listeners will be attentive.

7. They can read aloud sentences, phrases, and words that are useful in proving a point during story discussion, responding with the words of others to support their own ideas and viewpoints.

8. They can read aloud in an assessment situation, one-on-one with the teacher or diagnostician, without rehearsal and without the embarrassment of peers listening in. Adding uninvolved listeners to a testing situation will alter the character of the situation and skew the results.

9. They can read aloud findings from their research activities to other interested children. Perhaps different groups have explored various aspects of a theme or topic, and want to hear from each other to expand their knowledge. They can transfer their findings to overhead transparencies or large charts and share the information by reading aloud. They can read aloud inside the drama frame, using words that they have created through role-play, rules, statements, findings — or words they have found in

excerpts, letters, documents, tales. This role reading gives added strength to the oral interpretation; belief and commitment often transcend any limitation or difficulty with reading print.

10. They can read scripts (though good ones are difficult to find) aloud in small groups, first reading silently, then exploring the concepts, finding the voices. Better to leave concentrated teaching to whole-class activities. The groups can tape-record their scripts to help themselves further their interpretive work.

11. They can dramatize poems and excerpts using the words of others, but, through interpretive improvisation, bring to them movement and belief. These "minimal scripts" offer opportunity for partner, small group, and whole class exploration. Situations can be added, characters can be changed, music can be incorporated. The children may want to commit changes to memory, the ultimate act of oral interpretation.

12. They can chant, sing, shout, call, and respond alternate lines or sections of a story. At the conclusion of a particular theme or unit, they can read interesting or significant findings — poems that touched them, excerpts that made connections, quotations from novels that represent universal truths, personal writings from journals or writing folders that they feel will have special appeal for their class. The ritual of sharing and summarizing is vital to oral reading in many aspects of tribal life. We can incorporate this power in classroom teaching.

13. Readers' theatre is a technique that allows the children to dramatize narration — selections from novels, short stories, picture books, poems — instead of reading aloud scripted material.

    The children can have one person read the narration, others the dialogue speeches, or they can explore who should read which line. For example, a character who speaks dialogue may also read the information in the narration that refers to him or her. Several children can read narration as in a chorus.

14. Story theatre is another technique that allows children to dramatize material other than scripts. As well as interpreting the dialogue and the narration aloud, the participants can also play out all the actions and movements in the story. Simple narratives, such as those found in myth, fable, legend, and folktale from the oral tradition, are best suited for story theatre.

Reading aloud has been the lifeblood of our work for over thirty years. We read, they read, we read together, we echo each other, we make dialogue into script, we chant, we sing, we demonstrate, we share moments, we delight in words, we repeat, we whisper, we shout, we read and move our bodies, we read and clap our hands, we read to those who can't or don't, we read what they don't have or can't see, we read to reveal information we have found, we read to make a point, we read together as a ritual of belonging, we read from our memories, without print, we read to hear the sounds of language, we read to give others our own print ideas, we read to change direction and refocus, we read to bring together bits and pieces into broader themes, we read to find the voices deep within the well, we read to raise our own voices in tribute to literacy.

We read aloud what we've written, excerpts from other stories that we loved or wondered about, words that touch us or puzzle us, tales from before, stories about today and tomorrow, episodes from people's lives, poems that cry out for sounds in the air, letters from friends, stories about places where we have never wandered, stories about dogs and horses and mothers and grandads and eccentrics and children and school and city and countryside, stories of hope and death and wonder and fantasy. We read short stories and long stories and chapters that build up the tension for days. We read stories from album covers and music sheets, blurbs about writers from the backs of book jackets, titles, reviews, and recommendations. We read aloud, we fill the classroom with the voices of our ancestors, our friends, our authors, our poets, our records, our documents, our native people, our researchers, our journalists, our ad writers. We story aloud.

A Grade 7 class was working with us on a project to explore their need for emotional story connections as well as intellectual responses. We chose *I Am the Cheese* by Robert Cormier, a complicated novel with no straight narrative, but rather a random and yet cumulative series of transcripts between an interviewer and an interviewee. Because we were new to the class, we wanted to begin with a high comfort level, and we decided to work in small groups for the first hour-long session.

With six copies of the book, we were able to break into groups of five. Each group chose a reader who then read aloud the page we had marked, and no more. Then the books were closed while the members of each group discussed simply: "What is happening in your excerpt?" The transcripts are brief, minimal scripts, as in this sample:

*T:* Tell me about the telephone calls.
   *(10-second interval.)*
*A:* I have a feeling you already know about them. I have a feeling you know everything, even my blank spots.
*T:* Then, why should I make you go through it all? Why should I carry on this charade?
*A:* I don't know.
*T:* You disappoint me. Can't you think of the one person who will benefit?
   *(5-second interval.)*
*A:* Me. Me. Me. That's what you said at the beginning. But I never asked for it. I never asked to benefit by it.
   *(4-second interval.)*
*A:* I have a headache.
*T:* Don't retreat now. Don't retreat. Tell me about the phone calls your mother made.
   *(5-second interval.)*
*A:* There really isn't very much to tell.[8]

At first, the children had little to say, since the text gave almost nothing. However, as the discussion proceeded, questions began to arise, and the children began asking to hear the excerpt read again. It was a frustrating exercise, because they knew that inside the book might be all the answers to their questions. And yet they played along with us, working within what we had called a story puzzle. We then called all the groups together, and began to list on chart paper the information that each group had gleaned from its source. As the details emerged it was amazing to see the excellent reading that had been accomplished. However, one child asked to see another group's selection, and we then decided to have the various groups share with each other by having two groups exchange information at one time, until all groups had met each other. This took the remaining time in the first session.

At the beginning of the second session, the children volunteered information they had remembered from the previous session, as well as ideas they had discussed during the week. The list of suggestions was long, and many strong directions were beginning to emerge. However, they had not identified the exact relationship of the characters in the book. The period was over, and on the way out the door, two girls came running back into the room shouting: "It's the CIA in Washington! The boy's parents were assassinated!"

The entire class congregated around us demanding an answer, and we offered the six copies of the novel to volunteers, who snatched them from our hands.

The final session began and ended with their questions, about the book, abandoned children, interrogation, brainwashing, government control agencies, truth, and fiction. They had talked their way into making their own stories from one novel.

## Writing Our Own Stories

The connection between reading and writing has been evident in the classroom for a long time. but has it led to learning? What does writing do for the reader? What does reading do for the writer?

For most children, writing has been used as a follow-up to what has been read. Story patterns and story ideas have suggested the content of the resulting composition. The story has often been forgotten, acting only as a stimulus for beginning and structuring the ideas for writing. As well, many children have spent hours answering comprehension questions, but never consider the writing of their answers as an act of writing. As they retell, restate, find evidence for, sequence, infer, and judge, they are oblivious of how they are structuring and recording their answers. Even when taking up the questions, few teachers or children pay attention to the composition involved in the answers. New projects that are suggested, such as "book report-ing" activities, and all types of work cards and projects and centres that ask the child to respond to the story by writing, too often take the child away from the response mode to one of inventing, virtually a language activity. This is not to say that these types of activities are not of value. But they do not exhaust the possibilities of story as a wonderful springboard for writing: written responses to story *will* reveal and alter comprehension; follow-up storying activities *can* integrate language learning and help children to express, organize, and communicate their ideas and questions. All acts of languaging are interrelated, but story should hold a special place in the child's development. The writ-ing activities that promote story, interpret story, alter story, or generate other stories must be true learning situations for both the child as reader and the child as writer. The teacher must assist the child; the child must be storying through writing.

The problems involved in writing down stories are varied and complex. For many children, encoding the story in print seems an insurmountable task. Very few teachers put themselves through such rigorous activity. The students know they will be judged not just on their storying strength but on their ability to put it down in print. Might they then forego the story for the form? Is there a danger that their tellings will take second place to their concern with the formalities of print? Is it possible that in our attempts to teach writing we may destroy story? Can we maintain the integrity of story and still help children write? It is a complicated task.

What stories do children write down? Real ones from their own experiences; semi-real ones they have heard or latched onto; memories that filter through time; dreams that may seem very real; fantasies that carry them out and beyond the real world; fictions that let them take part in any event they can imagine or conjure up; literary stories of all types using all patterns — monologues, tall tales, legends, poems, dialogues, updates. Could writing our story be like painting our story, where the process is embedded inside the final product? It may be that edit-ing a story must be a separate process from storying, unless we can see revision as a continually changing version of our story. Can we retrain ourselves as teachers to listen to the stories that the children want to tell? Through pre-writing activities, we can enable and support them in the search for forms and structures for sharing their stories. There are so many reasons to write and revise. However, it is storying that we must be concerned with, that we must encourage and strengthen. Each child is a potential teller of tales.

Children's writing draws from the content of the stories they have met — concepts, characters, styles, and patterns — both consciously and unconsciously. They begin by borrowing, and then they manipulate the ideas and conventions of story. They can begin by borrowing events, themes, issues, words, patterns, and characters, and continue to expand their own story hoards. When they connect stories to the larger body of literature, children are developing their sense of story. Comparing several stories by one author or books on the same subject or theme, so that children can place what they have read or heard in relation to other stories, gives them the chance to develop personal preference and the ability to discern and critique. More is better. They are developing their story frames, widening their expectations of what a story can be, how it can be constructed, how it can develop.

The stories the children hear and read give them ideas for writing, and that writing in turn can be used for sharing their insights into the stories they have experienced. Revealing our understanding of a story through writing lets us then link two vital processes together so that we can share what is inside our minds. We verbalize and mediate our feelings in our writing. As children write their own versions they can then redefine through discussion and comparison in groups with others, they can become active storyers who begin to understand themselves as both readers and writers.

Today's writing curricula stress the active use of writing rather than exercises about writing. In some classrooms, traditional motivations for writing have dealt not with an inner compulsion or felt need, but only with the completion of creative writing tasks. When the writing is embedded in a context that has a personal significance for the writer, writing skills will be enhanced. The writer will work with genuine feeling and thoughtfulness, exploring meaning through both content and form.

Writing can be a language form in which engaged

148

writers/participants embody their feelings and ideas, learning not only to express themselves but to rethink, reassess, restructure, and re-examine themselves in the light of their own growth, perhaps even with an understanding of the reading audience and its needs. Children may begin to think of themselves as writers, controling the medium in order to find a way to say what they want to say to people they want to reach.

The children can use their imaginations to journey further into the story and let the meanings that accrue in the storying reveal themselves in their writings. As children try for a more complex imaginative understanding of what is happening in a story, their writing becomes more complex and their language deepens. Because writing may be read or listened to by others, there is a built-in reason to proofread and edit.

Drama can assist us in several ways in helping children write. The imaginative involvement that arises in drama can in turn be a powerful stimulus for writing. That writing can serve several different purposes in building and developing an imaginative thematic unit. The best language work grows over an extended period, during which children have time and incentive to work their way in to refocus and change directions; and to edit and present their creations to trusted and accepting others. By working in role, children are attempting to change perspective and move into inventive worlds and unfamiliar contexts. Because drama is an art-form that happens in reality as it progresses in fiction, the process is similar to composing in writing. The children build an imaginary world and become involved in what they are creating.

Within drama, the students can explore all the writing strategies — free writing, journals,interviews, brainstorming, lists, letter writing; creating announcements, proclamations, and petitions; reporting about events within the drama; designing advertisements and brochures; inventing questionnaires and important documents; and writing narrative stories that are part of or that are conjured up by the story told. As well, many opportunities are provided for collective writing, in which groups collaborate on a mutual enterprise. For example, they can cooperate in collecting data, organizing information, revising, and editing, all in a learning context.

In one class, the children were discussing the predicament that

149

George had found himself in in a story in the *George and Martha* series by James Marshall. The children decided to write advice to George, which indicates their involvement, both intellectual and emotional, with the story. Most of the selections begin in the first person, although there was no instruction from the teacher.

I advise you to make your own food so you won't say to each other I don't like this and go to restronts alot and if one of you are ill ask him or her what you would like and how they wont it made thats what I say.

I understand your problem you ought to tell Martha about the soup or just say I don't want that today. If you feel that way about Martha. Why don't you marry then it would be easyer to tell her don't you think. I am sure you will get along with each other. I would try some more flavors of soup it could be tasty.

You should not be angry you should tell them to be friends maybe marry live together. Or spend a holiday together. Buy presents for each other by happy enjoy life. Meet people. They should never disagree.

I advised George to tell Martha every time if there was any trouble. I advised Martha never to give George Split Pea Soup again.

I would advise you to spend more time with each other and to learn what each of you like and dislike.

All you have to do is to tell Martha the truth because she will find out later. You sould live together because will make a nice couple. Martha would make you cook.

I would tell them to get married or get engaged. Not to be just good friends get to know each other really well. And that's all there is to it.

A group of nine-year-olds had been working with Kermit Krueger's telling of the folktale "The Golden Swans". They had improvised the incident that occurs when the stranger in the story unknowingly kills a golden swan. The children decided cooperatively to force the stranger to build a statue in memory of the swan, and created these proverbs to be carved thereon:

Death to those who comes here to kill.

The hunter who killed our ansestors cared this.

The man who killed the swan has carved the swan for us.

This is a trubute to show what happened to the ansesters when one hunter came along an distroyed them. They were in the form of a swan.

Do not tuch the swans or els. Because they men so mytch to us.

Never kill a thing.

Those who kill our swans shall be put to work.

Those who kill in this village shall be punished.

To the passers and villages that live in the village. You have kill the swan and have done evil.

We do not kill. And those who do kill will do work and they will not finish until it is completely finished.

Never kill a golden swan without permission, for the story says never.

People who are near read *this*. This statue is a dead swan; it is alone for all to remember.

In the following letters by students playing the role of the protagonist in the tale, the children show strong role identification, as well as an understanding of the feelings of the hunter and the consequences of his deed. In their discussion they decided that the story was set in Vietnam. The letters vary between the formality of the hunter who has committed the crime and the informality of people away from home writing a friendly letter. This mix of the actual and the created indicates the negotiation of meaning that must be a part of the learning.

Dear brother

I have found this strange town with the name of Viet Nam
there is a story about some golden swans which are really
spirits when you grow up please come and you might even
see them. They were made by Indra's god come when you
are older.

Dear daughter and son,

I am writing to you to tell you I am ok. I am in Viet Nam
in a little village. It is very strange in this little village. Then
one day I was walking in a deep forest when I saw a lake
and some golden swans I ran and caught one. When I felt
it died. And the people of the village were angry with me.
I said I was sorry, but they still are angry. I have pondered
for many days, and I have thought of a idea. I have built
a statue of a swan, and the people have lost their angryness.

from your father,

p.s. Hope you are keeping well.

Dear Son

It is very strange in this place. I killed a golden swan and
all the towns people were very mad with me. I hope you
are ok. They played war with me for been a hunter because
they had no hunters in that land. I hope I will be coming
home soon. I just sit here thinking about the crime I caused.
I know no one here. I hope mum will send me clen clothes.

## Parallel Reading

Another follow-up activity children can engage in after a story
experience is to meet more stories that illuminate, clarify, or open
up the original narrative.

We may begin with one particular story with a class, but before
long, the children have found a dozen more, some hidden in
the recesses of their story minds, some discovered in the library,
some invented through storytelling sessions, and others created
collaboratively through story-building activities. As teachers, we
also add our own selections, some to be read or told aloud, others

to be left on a table to be read by volunteers. One story gives birth to a thousand.

In working with the following material, one class went through several steps.

A merman was caught at Orford in Suffolk during the reign of Henry II (1154-1189). He was imprisoned in the newly-built castle, did not recognize the Cross, did not talk despite torture, returned voluntarily into captivity having eluded three rows of nets, and then disappeared never to be seen again. That's what the chronicler Ralph of Coggeshall says in his "Chronicon Anglicanum."

Kevin Crossley-Holland,
*The Wildman*[9]

In small groups, round robin fashion, the children pretended the incident had been passed on in family stories. They recalled what they knew from their families about this "handed-down" incident. The storytelling was in the third person.

The groups created three tableaux in sequence which explained the origins of the "Wildman".

In pairs, the children improvised stories about the Wildman's appearance in the village. They also developed movement phrases which depicted a meeting between a villager and the Wildman. These phrases were developed into a dance study entitled "The Encounter".

The children visited the Wildman's world beneath the sea through Walt Whitman's poem, "The World below the Brine". They read it together chorally, then created the movement sequences that portrayed the passage from ocean depths to eventual emergence on land.

Kevin Crossley-Holland's retelling of *The Wildman* proved to be a very exciting discovery, for in many instances there were similarities between the children's retellings and that of a respected author. A timely retelling appeared for instance, in an anthology of poetry by Charles Causley, *Jack the Treacle Eater*: the ballad "Francesco de la Vega" provided a different kind of wild man story, but one right in line with the investigation of the children.

When the students of Larry Swartz's Grade 4/5 class entered

the room on the first day of school they were greeted by a display of thirty picture books from his collection that filled the book shelf along the front wall of the room. Larry was beginning the year with a humor theme, and after discussing what makes stories funny, he arbitrarily distributed one picture book to each student. Such authors as John Burningham, Anthony Browne, Tony Ross and Daniel Pinkwater were being introduced to the students within one hour of returning to school in September.

The students spent some time reading the books silently and then together discussed the merits of each book and whether it could be considered funny or not. A few students gave a brief retelling of the stories they had read and then the students were given a Reading Response journal in which, they were told, they would be recording their thoughts about the books that they would be reading throughout the year. Keeping Aidan Chambers's *Booktalk* in mind, Larry explained to the students that the journal was a place to discuss in writing what they liked, what they didn't like, what they were reminded of, what puzzled them, and what questions they might have about the books they'd be reading. He told them that he would give them some suggestions and questions that would help them use the journal effectively and explained that as the year went along, they could use this writing book as a place to share their reactions and connections to any novels, picture books, and poems that they'd be encountering.

To help structure the first entry, Larry wrote two questions on the board.

1. How did you enjoy the story?
2. How did the author and illustrator of the book tickle your funnybone?

Larry collected the journals of those who wished to submit them at this time, and began to write messages back to the students by making comments and raising questions in their journals. For one thing the students would quickly realize that their journal would have an audience and for another there was an opportunity for dialoguing about literature. Booktalk had begun.

On the second day of school, Larry once again distributed a new picture book to each student. This time, before reading the books, the students were told to imagine that they were going to be judges for a funny book contest and over the next few days they would decide which books were their favourites. The whole class discussed what criteria they would use to judge their books, as Larry recorded their points on the chalkboard.

For the second activity with these picture books, the students were divided into groups of five. This time, after the children read their books silently, they each presented their books to the rest of the group, perhaps retelling the story, referring to a particular funny picture, or giving an opinion on what appealed or didn't appeal to them. Larry was able to join in on three out of the six book conferences.

The third day began with Larry sharing the book *Where's Julius?* by John Burningham with the whole class to demonstrate some of the things that might be discussed in the groups. Together the class discussed favorite illustrations that had Julius digging holes to the other side of the world, washing hippopotomi, and watching rising sunsets. The children asked about the "strange" British foods such as roly poly pudding and potatoes in their jackets. They talked about the parents who kept taking Julius his food, and Larry asked why they thought Julius's father stopped serving him his dinner, demanding that "tonight we're having dinner at the table". To promote further reflection Larry asked the class whether they thought these adventures were really happening to Julius, and if not why did his parents keep serving him food? He also asked the students why it was easy for them to join in with the story when he read it aloud, pointing out the repeated structure Burningham used throughout the book. By taking the time to discuss illustrations, vocabulary, theme, and style, the students were given a model for discussing their own books back in their groups.

Each group was told that they would have to spend time choosing one book that they thought would be a suitable finalist for the funny book contest. The criteria, still displayed on the board, could be used as a reference for their decisions. If it was difficult to choose one book, they would have to consider how a decision could be reached.

After a fifteen-minute discussion, each group reported its favorite selection. The finalists were. . .

*The Great Blueness and Other Predicaments*, by Arnold Lobel
*We're Back!* by Hudson Talbot
*Where's Julius?* by John Burningham
*The Sixteen Hand Horse*, by Fred Gwynne
*Naughty Nigel*, by Tony Ross
*Lulu and the Flying Babies*, by Posy Simmonds

Over the next week, Larry read aloud one of the selections each day so that the whole class could experience the six selections. During the week all the picture books were made available to students to choose as they wished as other activities on the humor theme were introduced into the program.

As for the contest, after all six books were shared, a ballot was given to each student and a "winner" was declared.

An activity such as this that has the students discussing books introduces and promotes the type of learning atmosphere that Larry intends to build in his classroom.

1. The students were working in groups to share information, to ask questions and to make decisions.

2. The students were introduced to a variety of authors and stories. After hearing someone describe a book, many in the class chose to read that book on their own, or perhaps read others by the same author.

3. Because the students had to judge the books, and make connections between books and their own lives, they were invited to work beyond the literal and inferential stages of comprehension. The task demanded that they think critically. At the beginning, students commented that they liked the book "because it was funny," or because "the story was good." Such statements are just starting points for response. Through questioning and further dialoguing with peers and teacher, they were being called upon to revisit a book, to criticize it, and to respond meaningfully to it.

## Story Visuals

For many children, the visual arts (we include in this category drawing, painting, collage, work with construction paper, papier mâché, and so on) are their sole means of representing thoughts and feelings. Children who have no print power, who are unable to write responses — because of their lack of literacy development, anxiety, lack of self-worth, or attitude — can and often will express their ideas visually in a non-print medium. The results can then be used as "notes" or points for group discussion, or just as a personal expressive response. The teacher can observe what the child chooses to "say" — the details that seemed significant, the content of the art, the feeling that is suggested, the style used for representation. Through further discussion, in a student/teacher dialogue or in small groups, the child may further reveal and explain, and the teacher can help the child clarify, modify, support, and extend the story. Writing is a medium with strengths and weaknesses. Visual arts may offer a different mode of expression and communication, spontaneous and unedited, one that flows out of the story experience as a natural form.

Our concern here is the storying; artistic development is a by-product, not lesser than storying, but not the primary concern for our purposes. One simple strategy is to use collage to free children from the need for print or artistic skill. A Grade 4 classroom had a large supply of colorful magazines available for the following lesson. The teacher began by reading the nursery rhyme "Hannah Bantry" aloud.

Hannah Bantry
In the Pantry
Gnawing on a mutton bone,
How she gnawed it,
How she clawed it,
When she found herself alone.

As the teacher reread the poem, the children were asked to imagine Hannah in their minds — when she lived, what she looked like, what she was wearing, why she was eating in such a fashion, what she did, why she waited to be alone, why the lines had lived for so many years. Then, individually and silently, without conferring with each other, the children were to create a picture of Hannah Bantry, caught in the act, as if by a camera. They were to use collage — looking through magazines for pictures or pieces of pictures, ripping them out carefully and gluing them to a sheet of cardboard. The children were asked to use as many symbols as possible in creating their visuals, to represent Hannah's life with whatever images they thought could suggest and interpret it for a viewer.

When the portraits were complete, the children mounted their creations with masking tape across the blackboard. Then they examined all the pieces of art and began to notice similarities and differences.

As a class the children began to classify and categorize the faces: those that seemed frightened, those that appeared lonely, those that loved food, those that were happy, and so on. The children were examining responses to the story poem, building a world of personal interpretation and adding to their own singular visions by sharing perceptions, helping each other examine critically, and coming to understand the general principles of building bigger story worlds through interaction.

In this example of one child's collage of the father in *My Dad Lives in a Downtown Hotel* by Peggy Mann, you can see the interpretation he has created, a strong representation of that father; a picture story of what the child has thought and felt.

Children can respond to story visually through picture making, crafts and games, or film-making.

The teacher can provide materials for artistic work, and help children to think about their responses to a story in order to focus their questions and reactions through painting and modeling.

Collaborative efforts can draw children together as they plan and work through their ideas and feelings about the story. Sometimes the art can be used to further the story response — within a role, as illustration of the writing, as an opportunity to share perceptions. Picture books present a wonderful source for artistic response — the medium used, the style and format, and the point of view of the illustrator can all stimulate non-print activity.

One Grade 7 class, after reading and working with West Coast Indian tales about Sketco the Raven, created a film which they wrote and produced, dramatizing a mythic tale with human representation. They added dialogue after the film was complete, and shared the tale with other classes.

It is often said that television's popularity has resulted in children who are far more adept at responding to visual symbols

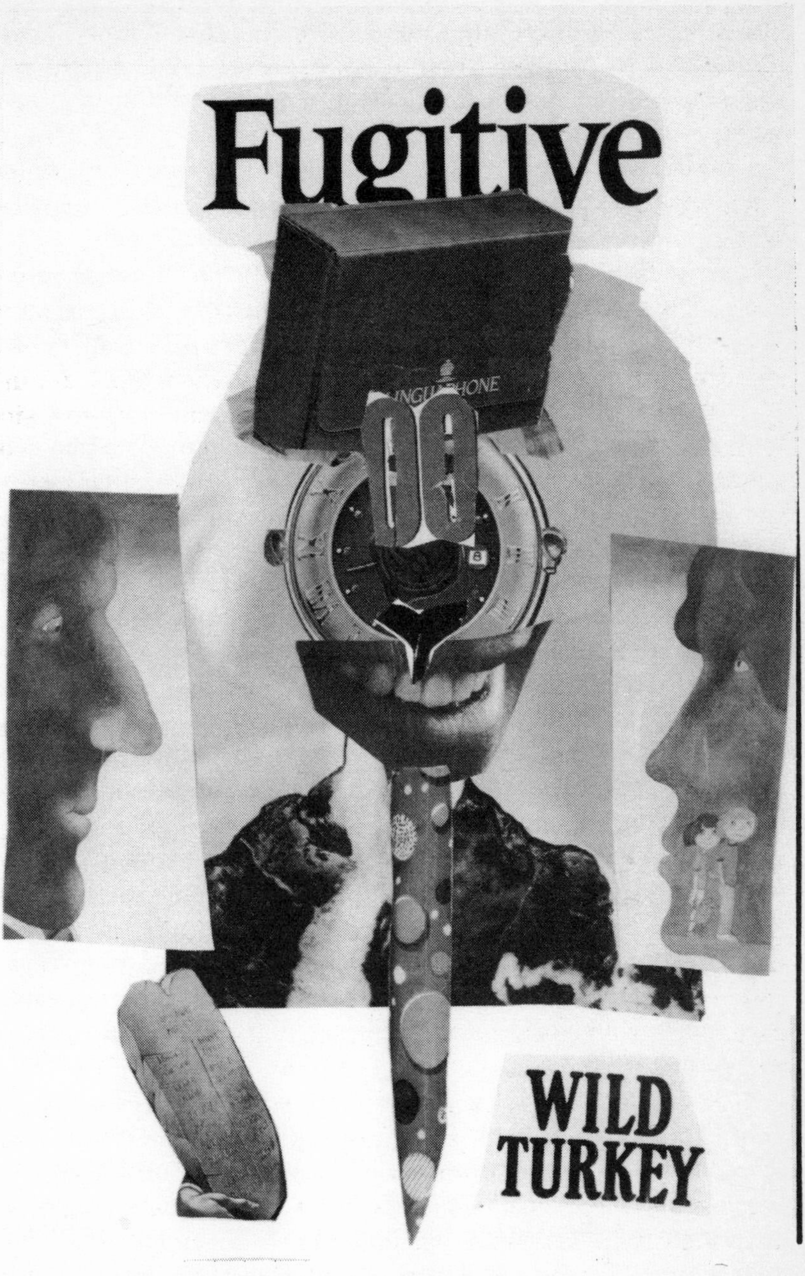
Fugitive
WILD
TURKEY

than to the written word. Whether this is true or not, visual response is an important means of interpreting the world. An appreciation of literature can be developed and motivation increased if we promote the constant harnessing of literature and the visual — television, film, cartoon, and the children's own work as picture-makers.

Children can assemble materials that relate to the story or stories they are exploring, objects mentioned in the text — collections, maps, facsimiles of journals, letters, advertisements, songs, clothes of the appropriate time. The research that the children collect can add to the context of the story either before or after its being shared, and the information presented can be an experience in itself.

Nursery rhymes can paint vivid pictures in a child's mind and may present opportunities for artistic expression. The bits and pieces of history and life that are brought to life in Mother Goose can stimulate all kinds of creative images for children. Often non-narrative, nonsensical, and higglety-pigglety, they use sounds and patterns to connote a cornucopia of meanings that can be tapped into as response material. While young children clap along, join in, and simply enjoy, older children can revisit the rhymes from childhood and begin to ponder their origins, their reasons for surviving, their stories — old and new. *Mother Goose Comes to Cable Street* by Rosemary Stones and Andrew Mann helps us to re-view these bits of heritage in a contemporary setting, altering our mind sets and our meaning frames.

Why is the book so effective? The original meanings are lost (if they ever meant anything in the first place), and yet the illustrations force a response by suggesting new meanings to the old ideas, by setting them down amid highrises and highways, shocking our sensibilities and our preconceptions, playing a game with our private worlds of meaning, teasing and twisting us into wondering.

This interpretive play is at the heart of the hundreds of illustrated versions of Mother Goose. The artist remembers a rhyme, rereads it, lets images flit across his or her mind, and begins to see the words in time and space. The response is visual, a natural outgrowth of the artist's life and mandate, and interpretive response is the outcome. For a long time to come, these poems will force artists to reflect and imagine, to crystallize and communicate their musings on the world of Mother Goose, creating anew the characters, the times in which they lived, and the events, imagined and real, that filled their lives. The pages will be full of eccentric old people, simple foods, wise parents, talking animals, and topsy-turvy worlds.

Some examples of the many illustrated versions of such stories are *Quentin Blake's Nursery Rhyme Book*, *The Random House Book of Mother Goose* by Arnold Lobel, and *Marguerite, Go Wash Your Feet* by Wallace Tripp.

Why deny child-artists, young respondees, this medium for storytelling? There are many literacies, and many modes of making meaning. Are artists not thinkers? Should we deprive young people of the game of thought, freed of print restrictions, problem-solving using symbol systems with paint and brush? Perhaps the little drawing at the bottom of the child's page of story-writing does not represent doodles or time fillers, but rather represents the heart of the response, a zap of inspired illumination. Children should have access to visual arts materials as media for their response repertoire. We want children to explore worlds of meanings in all dimensions. Their art can lead to new insights for artist and receiver, for the teacher-patron, and for the children who share with each other. Here are some ways you can bring visual storying into your classroom:

1. Visual arts can be used to prepare for a story session. A special puppet, a significant prop, a carefully executed illustration can set the scene, provide immediate involvement, and personalize the telling.

2. Children can sketch ideas as they read or listen to a story, or afterwards; their sketches can be used as jumping-off points for other activities, such as discussions, journals, comparisons of viewpoints, looking at sequences of story constructs.

3. A story told or shared without pictures to complement it can be the starting point for artistic interpretation. If the stress is on interpretation — an act of composing — rather than on the craftsmanship of the endeavor, the child will develop his own picture book, and take his place as a visual storyteller.

161

4. Children can create visuals cooperatively or collaboratively, negotiating their ideas and images, building on story response. Murals, dramas, cartoon strips, class-books, constructions using Lego toys, can all be part of the response.

5. Maps, charts, and graphs may lead to an in-depth analysis or synthesis of a story. As the children grapple with representing ideas, details, events, and significances, they may come to understand the power of story with graphic involvement.

6. An illustrated story may suggest to the reader a medium or technique to be used in the response. *Owl Lake* by Tejima cries out for print-making on heavy, quality paper. The content can be determined by the interpretation of the children. Will they revisit the owl family? Are birds of their region to be compared? Does Nature's unrelenting violence catch their fancy? Will they leave a margin around their pages, as Tejima does on some? Are they going to spread the wings across the whole of the paper? Will they hide the owls in the trees or create close-up views of their eyes? Are there other picture books, informational and fictional, to examine for assistance in developing a response? Teachers must provide materials, techniques, and direction; children will develop their own responses.

7. A visual timeline can be built by the readers to represent a tale. For example, incidents from the story can be drawn and hung on a clothesline in the sequence in which they occurred in the narrative.

8. The children can begin "versioning", developing their own story from a story they have heard or read. They can settle place, time, characters, details, mood, style, technique, displaying or binding strategies, designing a comparative study alone, in groups, or as a class.

9. The children can magnify one small detail or incident in a story and prepare a close-up view of *their* vision of it. It may be a vignette only briefly mentioned, or a place not described, or an incident just referred to in the story.

10. A story quilt can be created, each contributor adding one patch to form the whole.

11. Masks can be created for characters in the story to wear while enacting or improvising from the story. Part of a group can respond to what others are saying or reading, using the masks and movement to interpret the story words.

12. Pictures can accompany the stories created by the children themselves as they stand on the shoulders of stories they have heard or read. One child may illustrate another's work, causing the two students to share details of interpretation so that the story and illustrations are a collaborative effort.

. . . a word about drawings. Many people ask me why I seem to prefer drawings to words as a thinking medium for children. There are several reasons. Young children are not always very good at expressing their ideas in words and it would be a pity if their ideas were to be restricted by insisting that they use words. Again, words can sometimes be difficult to understand and interpreting the meaning behind them may become a matter of guesswork. Drawings, however, are clear and relatively unambiguous. To make a drawing you have to commit yourself to a definite idea: you cannot say 'the bricks are put in position more quickly than usual' in a drawing because you have to show exactly how this is done. There are more advantages. With a drawing the whole idea is visible all at once and you can work at it with addition, alteration, modification, change, etc. With words you have either to remember it all in your mind or else read through your description each time you want to see what you have got. It is significant that in a recent survey of inventive people the only uniform characteristic was their use of drawings and sketches in their thinking. Finally, there is the fact that children from disadvantaged backgrounds are often handicapped when it comes to the use of words. But preliminary work suggests that there is no such handicap with visual expression.

Edward de Bono,
*Children Solve Problems*[10]

## Celebrating Stories and Authors

In *Dear Mr. Henshaw*, Beverly Cleary mocks the reader/author interaction: Leigh Botts writes Mr. Henshaw for author information because of a school assignment. For four years, Leigh has handed in a book report on the same book, but now he contacts the author.

November 15

Dear Mr. Henshaw,

At first I was pretty upset when I didn't get an answer to my letter in time for my report, but I worked it out OK. I read what it said about you on the back of *Ways to Amuse a Dog* and wrote real big on every other line so I filled up the paper. On the book it said you lived in Seattle, so I didn't know you had moved to Alaska although I should have guessed from *Moose on Toast*.

When your letter finally came I didn't want to read it to the class, because I didn't think Miss Martinez would like silly answers, like your real name is Messing A. Round, and you don't have kids because you don't raise goats. She said I had to read it. The class laughed and Miss Martinez smiled, but she didn't smile when I came to the part about your favorite animal was a purple monster who ate children who sent authors long lists of questions for reports instead of learning to use the library.

Your writing tips were OK. I could tell you meant what you said. Don't worry. When I write something, I won't send it to you. I understand how busy you are with your own books.

I hid the second page of your letter from Miss Martinez. That list of questions you sent for me to answer really made me mad. Nobody else's author put in a list of questions to be answered, and I don't think it's fair to make me do more work when I already wrote a report.

Anyway, thank you for answering my questions. Some kids didn't get any answers at all, which made them mad, and one girl almost cried, she was so afraid she would get a bad grade. One boy got a letter from an author who sounded real excited about getting a letter and wrote such a long answer the boy had to write a long report. He guessed nobody ever wrote to that author before, and he sure wouldn't again. About ten kids wrote to the same author, who wrote one answer to all of them. There was a big argument about who got to keep it until Miss Martinez took the letter to the office and duplicated it.

About those questions you sent me. I'm not going to answer them, and you can't make me. You're not my teacher.

Yours truly,
Leigh Botts

P.S. When I asked you what the title of your next book was going to be, you said, Who knows? Did you mean that was the title or you don't know what the title will be? And do you really write books because you have read every book in the library and because writing beats mowing the lawn or shoveling snow?[11]

Authors and illustrators are worthy of respect and must be treated carefully by teachers and schools. The sadness of the continued use of book reports in place of response activities points out the need we have as teachers for ways of working alongside professional storymakers in developing our children's story sense. Authors cannot handle all the requests for speaking or for answering letters, and we must help our children show consideration and understanding for these authors when they are fortunate enough to meet them in person or correspond through letters. Preparation is necessary for promoting the learning in these situations.

Meeting an author, illustrator, poet, or storyteller is an exciting and motivating experience for children. With planning, such a meeting can become a story event, with invitations, promotion, organization, interviewing, discussion, and follow-up activities all being organized with the children. The children can use this "author awareness unit" to begin to understand the voice behind the words and/or pictures.

When children recognize professional authors as real people, they begin to see the writing of stories differently. They come to understand themselves as writers, and the authoring process is made accessible. The personal feelings that children develop from meeting authors promote further reading of selections by those authors, along with books on related themes. Stories are then seen as reflections of those who write them down, and children can see themselves as both readers and writers. We celebrate authors and storytellers and poets whenever and wherever possible.

It is important that as much teaching potential as possible be gleaned from the experience of meeting authors. As organizer and resource person, the teacher can arrange the visit (check with your board to find out about funding — many boards have access to grants to cover the costs of bringing in authors), and then begin the preparation with the children — locating the writings and making them available, finding sources of biographical information, helping children to create a list of significant questions for an interview, planning with the children for invitations and thank-you letters, working with the writings, exploring the content, style, and themes of the author, setting up displays that promote the author as writer for this celebration. Nothing is more demoralizing for an author than to be invited to a school where none of the children have read his or her work.

Jean Little is an international story star. Her novels, poems, short stories, and autobiographical works provide children with portraits of small town relationships that illuminate her life and ours. She shines as a story author and a storyteller in her work as an artist in the classroom. In this excerpt from a speech she made, Jean Little sums up what can happen in a single author visit. But the excerpt is also about the power of story, and a fitting way to end this chapter.

Let me finish by celebrating some kids I met when I was on a tour for Children's book Week. Since I have never toured Manitoba for the Centre, let's say it happened there. The names have been changed to protect the privacy of the children involved.

We were late arriving. We had had car trouble en route. The library consultant was waiting for us, all in a swivet, because we were to have dinner at the home of one of the fifth-grade teachers and we were already an hour late. The library lady and I went at top speed down a few streets and pulled up before a private home.

We met our hostess, apologized at length, made sure my guide dog was polite to her chihuahua and sat down to a marvelous dinner. Our hostess did not say much. She simply plied us with mouthwatering dishes. When, replete, we returned to the living room, the library consultant and I got onto the debate about bibliotherapy. Having been called a bibliotherapist more than once and being well aware that it was not meant as a compliment, I rushed to attack "mere" bibliotherapy. The library consultant and I were busily agreeing how terrible a thing it was when our hostess, Miss Cameron, joined us. As I wound down momentarily, my hostess announced, "I don't know about that. All I do know is that you have worked a miracle in my classroom."

"I did?" I said weakly.

"Yes," she said. "And I'm really glad you are here so that I can tell you about it in person."

Then she told us the following story.

That September, a boy named Simon had arrived in her class. She had known he was coming and she had dreaded having him because his reputation had preceded him. Everyone who had ever taught him agreed that he was impossible. He resisted learning anything. He seemed in a daze, rarely spoke to anyone, never volunteered an answer. When asked a direct question, he either sat mute or muttered, "I don't know." Although everyone in the class had long since moved from printing to cursive writing, Simon stubbornly went on printing everything. When he was supposed to bring a book, he simply did not. He lived alone with his father.

Miss Cameron, like every teacher before her, had been at her wit's end trying to reach this child.

Then the library consultant arrived with a copy of *From Anna*. She told Miss Cameron that an author was coming, that sixteen members of her class of twenty- eight students would be able to attend the author's presentation and it would mean so much more if they had been introduced to one of the books the woman had written. Why not read *From Anna* aloud to the kids?

Miss Cameron, who had never heard tell of this writer from Ontario, dutifully began reading a chapter or two every day. She had found this year's class to be a pretty rowdy bunch and she was pleased to discover that they settled down when storytime rolled around. Then, one day, she happened to glance over at Simon. She was astonished. He was listening! Simon — who never listened.

She went on reading but continued to glance his way every so often. He was watching her intently, his usually-blank face alert and responsive.

They finished the second-last chapter on a Thursday afternoon. As she closed the book, she told the children that there was only one chapter left and that they would finish it the next day. A few minutes later, as she was bending over some work on her desk, she heard a voice say, "Miss."

She looked up. Simon was standing there, his eyes fixed upon her face.

"Yes, Simon," she said, trying not to show her surprise at his actually starting a conversation.

"Miss," he repeated huskily, "what are you going to do with the book when you've finished it?"

Speaking as matter-of-factly as she could, she said, "Well, I suppose I'll put a card in the back and then anyone who wants to may borrow it."

"Can I have it?" Simon asked.

"Certainly," his teacher said. "You are the first one to ask so you can be the first one to take it out."

The next day, she gave it to him. When Monday came, he arrived with it clutched in his hand. Everywhere he went that day, *From Anna* went with him. She could hardly believe it.

She decided to have the class write book reviews of the story to present to me.

"Write down what you liked best about the story," she instructed.

"If we didn't like something, should we put that in?" one of the other boys asked.

Before the teacher had a chance to reply, Simon whirled around and glared at the other child.

"Not like it!" he cried. "I LOVE that book."

The whole class stared at his flushed face in amazement. Nobody had ever heard Simon speak passionately about anything. Nothing more was said about not liking the book. They all began to write their reviews.

Some wrote half a page. Most wrote a page or two. Simon wrote three-and-a-half pages. His review mentioned every moment of tenderness between Anna and her father in the early chapters.

"Then Papa gave Anna a big hug . . ." it read. And a line or two later, "Then Papa gave Anna's hand a warm squeeze."

Simon also mentioned Miss Williams, the teacher who liked and encouraged Anna.

They wrote a rough draft and then copied it out 'nicely' to give to me. As Miss Cameron passed Simon's desk, he looked up at her, his face alight.

"I'm writing this, Miss," he told her. "I'm not printing. I'm writing this for Miss Little."

But only sixteen children could go to the Public Library to see and hear me. Who would get to go? Simon was worried. So were the rest. How was Miss Cameron going to choose?

The speech teacher, who visited the school that day, decided to help. She got each of the children to write down why he or she wanted to be among the lucky ones picked to attend the Author Visit. When they had all done so, each one read his or her reasons onto a tape which would be presented to me along with the book reviews.

Miss Cameron was reading *Listen for the Singing* to the class. Simon was still listening.

"I want to go because I never saw an otter," Lucy said.

"I think I should be picked because I have never met a talented person," said Donald.

"I want to see the dog," Randy said. "He is a Seeing Eye dog. They are extremely clever and excellent. They keep the person from getting hit by cars or trucks."

To Randy, the writer's dog was what mattered. He did not express any desire to see the author.

Then came Simon's voice, husky with feeling.

"I want to go to see Jean Little because I love her books very much," he said. "It would be the thrill of a lifetime . . . I am BEGGING you . . . PLEASE . . . let me go."

As Miss Cameron told me this story, I could feel my throat tightening. I blinked away tears.

"Well," I said, "even if it comes to nothing, it is wonderful that he has had such a joyous experience with one book . . "

Miss Cameron interrupted me.

"But it hasn't come to nothing," she told me emphatically. "When we finished *Listen for the Singing*, the same thing happened. And he's writing now and talking. He's come to life, in a way. He is a changed boy. I told you, you worked a miracle in my classroom."

That night, I lay awake in our hotel room thinking about Simon. In the morning, I would meet him, Miss Cameron had told me, because he had been chosen to give me the tape they had made. She herself would not be there. She was sending the supply teacher with the sixteen chosen children. She, their teacher, was staying behind with the twelve unlucky ones. I thought about that. And, suddenly, the whole story started making more sense. Although I knew that a book could mean a great deal to a child, no boy like Simon is so transformed by one novel. In my book, Anna, who is, like Simon, an unresponsive and difficult child, gets a teacher who shows her that she matters. And, with the encouragement of Miss Williams, Anna slowly comes out of her shell and dares to smile and make friends. Miss Cameron, I decided, was the Miss Williams in Simon's life. And when he heard about Anna, prickly, closed in, a failure loved only by her father, actually changing into a different Anna, he looked at Miss Cameron and decided to risk it himself. Perhaps not consciously. But I believed that that must have been how it had come about.

As I made my speech, I waited for the moment when Simon would present the cassette. But when the time came, a beaming girl handed it to me instead. How she got it away from him I could not inquire. It would have required too much explanation.

Quite a story. It made the whole tour worth while. It made all the tours in the future mean more.

But that isn't the end of it.

I came home and listened to the tape. I heard twenty-eight

ten-year-old children saying why and how much they longed to be chosen to go to see the lady who wrote *From Anna*. And I had no idea which twelve had had to stay behind.

It probably happens frequently. But it shouldn't. Four out of thirty being chosen is one thing; sixteen out of twenty-eight is quite another. It seemed cruel.

And I had all their names and their reasons for wanting to see the "otter". I wrote them a letter, calling each child by name and answering questions they said they wanted to ask me. I thought about Simon responding to Anna's story with such fierce delight and I sent the class a copy of *The Secret Garden*, telling them to get Miss Cameron to read it to them in the dead of winter. It had been the book that had meant most to me in my childhood, the most magical book I knew. I wrote four pages single-spaced and I enclosed a picture of Zephyr [her seeing-eye dog] in case Randy had been one of the twelve who did not get to come that day. It was not at all like writing to the class-sets of demanding letters. The children in Miss Cameron's class had not asked me for anything. They had given to me instead by loving my Anna so much.

And that still is not the end of the story. That fifth-grade class had experienced the death of one of their classmates before I visited their town. The day before my letter arrived Lucy's mother died of multiple sclerosis. The next morning, Miss Cameron told the class what had happened. Sadness filled the room. The rowdy class was too quiet and the teacher's heart ached for them as she watched them trail out for recess. Then she went to the Office to collect her mail and found my letter waiting. She sent me another tape to tell me about it.

"When they came in again," she told me, "despair turned to hope, sadness to joy. I read the letter aloud to them and, when I came to the end, they said, 'Oh, Miss, read it again.' So I did."

She took a copy to the little girl whose mother had died. And when the child searched for and found her name, her face lighted up with amazed delight.

They reminded her, right after Christmas, that I had told

them to get her to read *The Secret Garden* to them "in the dead of winter." The day she made the tape for me, they had finished Chapter Three. And over a month after she had sent them all home with a copy of the letter, they had a lesson on letter-writing. When they spoke of my letter, she asked them how many of them still had it. They gave her looks of pained surprise as all twenty-eight hands went up. Many of them had it by their bed and read it before they went to sleep. Some of them had persuaded their parents to buy them copies of my books and they kept their letters inside their Jean Little books.

It is a moving story. But please notice this one point. Simon was not transformed because he was told he had to read a book by a Canadian author and write her a letter. He began simply to listen to a story. Because he had a loving teacher, he found an extra blessing in it. I was never asked to write a letter. I wrote it freely because so many of them did not get to the author visit.

Although Canadian writers have gone out on tour for years, there had not been an author in that town before I came.

We must remember this fact: all over Canada are children who will never get to attend an author visit. I would send each of them a copy of *The Secret Garden* if I could. Since I can't, I want to write stories for them, the very best stories I can. When I walk in and make a speech, I am entertaining. The kids like it. but my heart cannot speak to theirs the way Anna's story spoke to Simon. I can only give that deeply of myself through my writing. If I am to reach more of Canada's young readers, I must stop being a "real-live-author" and go back to being a working writer. And how I hope and pray that in every class where there is a Simon there will also be a Miss Cameron who will read books out loud, my books, Barbara Smucker's and Marilyn Halvorson's, Claire MacKay's and Brian Doyle's and Kit Pearson's and Janet Lunn's, Ian Wallace's and Kevin Major's. And *Mary Poppins*, don't forget, and *Winnie the Pooh*, and *Playing Beattie Bow* and *Charlotte's Web* and *Come Sing, Jimmy Jo*. If only she is there, Canada's young readers, whether or not they can sound out every word, will have books to love. They will be offered a bequest of wings. They will be given invitations to joy.[12]

172

# Final Thoughts

Jean Little is right, of course. Stories are invitations to joy, and we cannot be grateful enough for our time spent experiencing and exploring stories with young people. It has been a constant quest to find the most appropriate story for a group at a given moment, and a continuing adventure developing significant response activities that would lead into the story and into the lives of the children, both at once.

The stories of children live beside the stories of their families, alongside the stories of their friends, and in the shadows of the stories authored and transcribed by others. We cannot value one over the other. Each and all are part of the storying world that we will inhabit from birth to death.

The place called school represents a fine locus for some of these stories, where we can discover and share and build stories together, bonds of narrative that link us inextricably. For many children, the stories in print that we bring them may have to do for their lives. Others will continue to fill their story bags until they need steamer trunks to contain them. It takes so many stories to become human — some spill out, some are forgotten, others only remain as bits and pieces. But no matter. In the sifting and the sorting of our story lives, we will all the time be developing our story sense, and as we retell one from memory, the remnants of others will haunt the present one and color it with hues unimagined. In the museums of our minds, the stories will touch each other, rub against each other, alter shape and substance, mix metaphor and symbol, become the ordinary and the fabulous.

We celebrate the children who teach us anew every time we story with them.

We celebrate the teachers who plunge into story pools with children.

We celebrate the authors and illustrators who write down, retell, invent, and illuminate stories from and for all people.

But most of all, we sing the praises of the story — that most simple and complex creation of all the arts, resonating from caves and echoing from the moons of distant planets. We are all part of the story tapestries of our tribes, our threads woven into yours, each tale embroidered with the strands of others, for all time.

A man wanted to know about mind, not in nature, but in his private large computer. He asked it (no doubt in his best Fortran), "Do you compute that you will ever think like a human being?" The machine then set to work to analyze its own computational habits. Finally, the machine printed its answer on a piece of paper, as such machines do. The man ran to get the answer and found, neatly typed, the words:

THAT REMINDS ME OF A STORY[13]

# Notes

## Introduction

[1] Harold Rosen, "Stories of Stories: A Postscript by Harold Rosen", in *And None of It Was Nonsense*, by Betty Rosen (London: Scholastic, 1988).

[2] Kathryn Morton, "Why Stories Matter", *New Times Book Review*, December 23, 1984.

## Chapter 1

[1] Miroslav Holub, "Napoleon", in *Gangsters, Ghosts and Dragonflies*, by Brian Patten (London: Pan Books Ltd., 1983).

[2] Natalie Babbitt, "My Love Affair with the Alphabet", in *Once Upon a Time* (New York: G.P. Putnam & Sons, 1986).

[3] Donald Fry, *Children Talk about Books: Seeing Themselves as Readers* (Milton Keynes: Open University Press, 1985).

[4] Carlos Fuentes, as quoted in *People Magazine*, October 14, 1988.

[5] Aidan Chambers, *Introducing Books to Children* (London: Heinemann, 1983).

[6] Frances Hodgson Burnett, *The Little Princess* (New York: Lippincott, reprinted 1972).

[7] Kornei Chukovsky, *From Two to Five*, translated by Miriam Morton (Los Angeles: University of California Press, 1963).

[8] Patricia Scott, *Sharing Stories: Storytelling and Reading Aloud* (Tasmania: Piglet Publications, 1979).

[9] Katherine Paterson, *Gates of Excellence* (New York: E.P. Dutton, 1988). A charming book of essays and speeches by the noted author of fine novels for young people.

[10] Robert Coles, *The Call of Stories* (Boston: Houghton Mifflin, 1989).

[11] Aidan Chambers, *Introducing Books to Children* (London: Heinemann, 1983).

[12] James Britton, *Language and Learning* (Harmondsworth: Penguin, 1970). The most important book on teaching language that we have read.

[13] Valerie Martin, "Waiting for the Story to Start" in the *New York Times*, February 16, 1988.

[14] Jean Little, *Hey World, Here I Am* (Toronto: Kids Can Press, 1987).

[15] Trina Shart Hyman, "Little Red Riding Hood", in *Once Upon a Time* (New York: G.P. Putnam & Sons, 1986).

[16] Kieran Egan, *Teaching as Storytelling* (London, Ontario: The Althouse Press, 1987).

[17] Maurice Saxby, *When John and Judy Don't Read* (New South Wales: Primary English Teachers Association, 1978).

[18] Bill Martin Jr., "A Memoir", in *Children's Literature in the Reading Program*, edited by Bernice Cullinan (Newark, Delaware: The International Reading Association, 1987).

## Chapter 2

[1] John Agard, "Mouth Open Story Jump Out" in *Say It Again, Granny!* (London: The Bodley Head, 1986). A collection of Caribbean poems written in dialect.

[2] Betty Rosen, *And None of It Was Nonsense* (London: Scholastic, 1988).

[3] Wolfgang Iser, *The Act of Reading* (London: Routledge and Kegan Paul, 1978).

[4] Margaret Meek, "A Time to Wonder", in *Puffin Projects and Primary Schools* (Hamondsworth: Penguin, 1971).

[5] Harold Rosen, "Stories of Stories: A Postscript by Harold Rosen" in *And None of It Was Nosense* (London: Scholastic, 1988).

[6] Julius Lester "The Beechwood Staff", in *Horn Book*, April, 1984.

[7] Geoff Fox and Michael Ber.ton, *Teaching Literature from Nine to Fourteen* (Oxford: Oxford University Press, 1985).

[8] William Steig, *Brave Irene* (New York: Farrar Straus Giroux, 1986).

[9] Kevin Crossley-Holland, "The Mule", in *British Folktales* (London: Orchard Books, 1987).

[10] Dorothy Heathcote, "Of These Seeds Becoming", in *Education Drama for Today's Schools*, edited by R. Baird Shuman (Metuchen, N.J.: The Scarecrow Press, Inc., 1978).

[11] Bill Martin, Jr. has described the power of story in the lives of children eloquently in his teaching notes to his language arts series *The Sounds of Language* (New York: Holt Rinehart Winston, 1970).

[12] Joan Aiken, "On Imagination", in *Innocence and Experience*, edited by Barbara Harrison and Gregory Maguire (New York: Lothrop, Lee and Shepard, 1987).

[13] Charles Reasoner has developed an excellent series of activities for introducing and extending reading in his manuals for Dell Yearling Paperbacks. See *Bringing Children and Reading Together* (New York: Dell, 1979).

[14] Linda Williams, *The Little Old Lady Who Wasn't Afraid of Anything* (New York: Crowell, 1986).

[15] Anne Pellowski, *The World of Storytelling* (R.R. Bowker & Co., 1977).

[16] Iona and Peter Opie, *Children's Games in Street and Playground* (Oxford: Oxford University Press, 1980), and *The Singing Game* (Oxford, 1985).

[17] Alan Newland's classroom is described in the journal *Language Matters*, #2 & 3, 1988, edited by Myra Barrs, Webber Row Teacher's Centre, Webber Row, London, SE1 8QW.

[18] Robert Coles, *The Call of Stories* (Boston: Houghton Mifflin, 1989).

[19] Shel Silverstein, "Forgotten Language", in *Where the Sidewalk Ends* (New York: Harper & Row, 1976).

[20] Wayne Booth, "Narrative as a Mould of Character", in *A Telling Exchange*, the report of the 17th Conference of Inner City Schools, University of London, Institute of Education, 1983.

## Chapter 3

[1] Langston Hughes, "Aunt Sue's Stories", in *The Dream Keeper and Other Poems* (New York: Alfred A. Knopf, 1986).

[2] Ted Hughes, "Myth and Education", in *Writers, Critics and Children* (London: Heinemann, 1976).

[3] Honor Arundel writing in *Author's Choice* (London: Hamish Hamilton, 1973).

[4] Bill Martin, Jr., "A Memoir", in *Children's Literature in the Reading Program*,

edited by Bernice Cullinan (Newark, Delaware: International Reading Association, 1987).

[5] Jane Yolen quotes this Maori tale in her introduction to *Favorite Folktales from around the World* (New York: Random House, 1986).

[6] Ibid.

[7] David Booth, "Owl Trouble", in the language arts series *Colours* (Toronto: Longman, 1972).

[8] Roger Abrahams, "Why Hens Are Afraid of Owls", in *Afro American Folktales* (New York: Pantheon, 1985).

[9] Adopted from the work of L.F. Ashley, "Aspects of Animal Tales", in *English Quarterly*, Vol. XI, #3, Fall 1978.

[10] Janet Hill, "Discovering Books: The Adult's Role", in *Puffin Projects and Primary Schools* (Harmondsworth: Penguin, 1971).

[11] Aidan Chambers, *Booktalk* (London: The Bodley Head, 1985).

[12] Liz Johnson and Cecily O'Neill, eds., *Dorothy Heathcote: Collected Writings on Educational Drama* (London: Hutchinson, 1984).

[13] Beverly Korbrin, *Eyeopeners* (Harmondworth: Penguin, 1988).

[14] Fay Blostein's books are excellent sources of thematic groupings of novels for young adults. *New Paperbacks for Young Adults, Invitations, Celebrations,* and *Connections* are all published by The Ontario Library Association, Toronto, 1979-1988.

[15] Jane Yolen, *Touch Magic* (New York: Philomel, 1981).

[16] G.K. Chesterton is quoted by Nicholas Tucker in *The Child and the Book* (Cambridge: Cambridge Press, 1981).

[17] Jane Yolen, *Touch Magic.*

[18] Jane Yolen, *Touch Magic.*

[19] Richard Chase, "The Big Toe", in *American Folk Tales and Songs* (New York: Signet Key Books, 1956).

[20] Ian Serraillier, "The Vistor", in *I'll Tell Your a Tale* (Harmondsworth: Puffin, 1976).

[21] Iona Opie, ed., *Tail Feathers from Mother Goose* (London: Walker Books, Ltd., 1988).

[22] Michael Rosen, "Shut Your Mouth When You're Eating", in *Quick, Let's Get Out of Here* (Harmondsworth: Puffin, 1985).

[23] Judith Nicholls, "Searcher", from the series of poems "Moses", in *Magic Mirror* (London: Faber & Faber, 1985).

[24] Jill Paton Walsh, *A Parcel of Patterns* (New York: Farrar Straus Giroux, 1985).

**Chapter 4**

[1] John Agard, "The Older the Violin the Sweeter the Tune" in *Say It Again, Granny!* (London: The Bodley Head, 1986).

[2] Charlotte Huck et al., *Children Literature in the Elementary School* (New York: Holt Rinehart Winston, 1987).

[3] Michael Ondaatje, *In the Skin of a Lion* (Toronto: McClelland and Stewart, 1987).

[4] Dorothy Heathcote.

[5] Jack Thompson, *Understanding Teenagers' Reading* (Sydney, Australia: Methuen, 1987).

[6] From a speech by Harold Rosen in Chicago at the annual convention of the International Reading Association, 1982.

[7] Gordon Wells, *The Meaning Makers* (London: Heinemann, 1986). An

extremely significant book on the role of talk in developing literacy in young children.

[8] Maurice Saxby, *When John and Judy Don't Read* (New South Wales: PETA, 1978).

[9] Arthur Yorinks, review in the *New York Times*, November 8, 1987.

[10] Margaret Mahy, *17 Kings and 42 Elephants* (New York: Dial, 1987).

[11] Walter de la Mare, "Song of the Mad Prince", in *Peacock Pie* (London: Faber, 1980).

[12] Paul Brock writing in *Teaching Literature* (New South Wales: PETA, 1983).

[13] Charles Causley, "Charity Chadder", in *Early in the Morning* (London: Viking Kestrel, 1986).

## Chapter 5

[1] This is the opening section of a traditional Ashanti African folktale.

[2] Aidan Chambers, *Booktalk* (London: The Bodley Head, 1985).

[3] Cynthia Rylant, *When I Was Young in the Mountains* (New York: E.P. Dutton, 1982).

[4] Edward Lowbury, "The Huntsman", in *Poems for Over 10-year-olds*, edited by Kit Wright (London: Viking Kestrel, 1984).

[5] Richard Edwards, "Our Pond", in *The Word Party* (Harmondsworth: Puffin, 1987).

[6] Connie and Harold Rosen, *The Language of Primary School Children* (Harmondsworth: Penguin, 1973).

[7] Cecily O'Neill, "The Wild Things Go to School", in *Drama Contact*, the Journal of the Council of Drama in Education, Toronto (Autumn, #12, 1988).

[8] Robert Cormier, *I Am the Cheese* (New York: Dell, 1977).

[9] Kevin Crossley-Holland, "The Wildman", in *British Folktales* (London: Orchard Books, 1987).

[10] Edward de Bono, *Children Solve Problems* (Harmondsworth: Penguin, 1972).

[11] Beverly Cleary, *Dear Mr. Henshaw* (New York: Dell, 1983).

[12] This excerpt is from a speech given by Jean Little, "Invitations to Joy", for the Canadian Children's Book Centre, Annual Lecture #1, 1988.

[13] Gregory Bateson, *Mind and Nature* (New York: Bantam, 1988).

# Bibliography

Abrahams, Roger, "Why Hens Are Afraid of Owls" in *Afro American Folk Tales* (New York: Pantheon, 1985).

Adams, Richard, *Watership Down* (London: Rex Collings, 1972).

Agard, John, *Say It Again, Granny!* (London: The Bodley Head, 1986).

Ahlberg, Allan, *The Mighty Slide* (London: Viking, 1988).

Ahlberg, Allan and Janet, *Each Peach Pear Plum* (London: Viking, 1979).

----------, *The Jolly Postman* (London: Viking, 1984).

Aiken, Joan, *The Moon's Revenge* (London: Jonathan Cape, 1987).

Aldan, Nowlan, "The Invisible Boy", in *Nine Micmac Lengends* (Hantsport, N.S.: Lancelot, 1983).

Andersen, Hans Christian, *The Wild Swans*. Illustrated by Angela Barrett. English version by Naomi Lewis. (London: Ernest Benn Ltd., 1984).

----------, *The Wild Swans*. Illustrated by Helen Stratton. (London: Hutchinson, 1986).

Andrews, Jan, *Very Last First Time*. Illustrated by Ian Wallace. (Toronto: Groundwood, 1985).

Anno, Mitsumasa, *Anno's Journey* (New York: Philomel, 1978).

Ardema, Verna, *Princess Gorilla and a New Kind of Water* (New York: Dial, 1988).

Arundel, Honor, *Author's Choice* (London: Hamish Hamilton, 1973).

Ashley, L.F., "Aspects of Animal Tales", in *English Quarterly*, Vol. XI, #3, Fall 1978.

Babbitt, Natalie, "The Rose and the Minor Demon", in *The Devil's Storybook*. (New York: Farrar, Strauss, 1974).

----------, "My Love Affair with the Alphabet", in *Once upon a Time* (New York: G.P. Putnam & Sons, 1986).

Baker, Jeannie, *Where the Forest Meets the Sea* (New York: Greenwillow, 1987).

Bang, Molly, *Dawn* (New York: Morrow, 1983).

Bateson, Gregory, "That Reminds Me of a Story", in *Mind and Nature* (New York: Bantam, 1988).

Baylor, Byrd, *Everybody Needs a Rock* (New York: Scribners, 1974).

Bell, Clare, *Ratha's Creature* (New York: Atheneum, 1983).

Berry, James, *Ananci Spiderman* (London: Walker, 1988).

Bierhorst, John, *Doctor Coyote* (Toronto: Macmillan, 1987).

Blake, Quentin, *Quentin Blake's Nursery Rhyme Book* (London: Jonathan Cape, 1983).

Blos, Joan, *Brothers of the Heart*. (New York: Scribner, 1985).

Blostein, Fay, *Connections* (Toronto: Ontario Library Association, 1988).

----------, *Invitations, Celebrations* (Toronto: Ontario Library Association, 1980).

----------, *New Paperbacks for Young Adults: 1 & 2* (Toronto: Ontario Library Association, 1979, 1981).

Booth, David, "Owl Trouble", in *Colours* (Toronto: Longman, 1972).

----------, *Til All the Stars Have Fallen*. Illustrated by Kady MacDonald Denton. (Toronto: Kids Can Press, 1989).

Booth, Wayne, "Narrative as a Mould of Character", in *A Telling Exchange*, report of the 17th Conference of Language in Inner City Schools (University of London, Institute of Education, 1983).

Briggs, Katherine, "Mr. Fox", in *British Folktales* (New York: Random House, 1977).

Briggs, Raymond, *Jim and the Beanstock* (London: Cavard, 1980).

----------, *Snowman* (London: Hamish Hamilton, 1978).

Brighton, Catherine, *Hope's Gift* (New York: Faber, 1988).

Britton, James, *Language and Learning* (Harmondsworth: Penguin, 1970).

Browne, Anthony, *A Walk in the Park* (London: Hamish Hamilton, 1977).

----------, *Gorilla* (London: Julia MacRae Books, 1983).

----------, *Piggybook* (New York: Knopf, 1986).

Burnett, Frances Hodgson, *The Little Princess* (New York: Lippincott, reprinted 1972).

Burningham, John, *Grandpa* (London: Jonathan Cape, 1987).

----------, *Where's Julius* (London: Jonathan Cape, 1988).

Carrick, Carol, *Patrick's Dinosaurs*. Illustrated by Donald Carrick. (New York: Clarion Books, 1984).

----------, *What Happened to Patrick's Dinosaurs?* Illustrated by Donald Carrick. (New York: Clarion Books, 1986).

Carrick, Donald, *Harald and the Giant Knight* (New York: Clarion Books, 1982).

Carson, Jo, *Stories I Ain't Told Nobody Yet* (London: Orchard Books, 1989).

Causley, Charles, "Charity Chadder", in *Early in the Morning* (London: Viking Kestrel, 1986).

----------, "Francesco de la Vega", in *Jack the Treacle Eater* (London: Macmillan, 1987).

Chambers, Aidan, *Booktalk* (London: The Bodley Head, 1985).

----------, *Introducing Books to Children* (London: Heinemann, 1983).

Chase, Richard, "The Big Toe", in *American Folk Tales and Songs* (New York: Signet Key Books, 1956).

Chukovsky, Kornei, *From Two to Five*. Translated by Miriam Morton. (Los Angeles: University of California Press, 1963).

Cleary, Beverly, *Dear Mr. Henshaw* (New York: Dell, 1983).

Cole, Brock, *The Giant's Toe* (New York: Farrar Straus Giroux, 1986).

Coles, Robert, *The Call of Stories* (Boston: Houghton Mifflin, 1989).

Cooper, Susan, *The Selkie Girl* (New York: Margaret K. McElderry Books, 1986).

Cormier, Robert, *I Am the Cheese* (New York: Dell, 1977).

Crossley-Holland, Kevin, "The Mule" and "The Wildman", in *British Folktales* (London: Orchard Books, 1987).

deBono, Edward, *Children Solve Problems* (Harmondsworth: Penguin, 1972).

De Jong, Meindert, *The Wheel on the School* (New York: Harper & Row, 1954).

De La Mare, Walter, "Song of the Mad Prince", from *Peacock Pie* (London: Faber, 1980).

De Regniers, Beatrice Schenk, *Little Sister and the Month Brothers* (New York: Clarion Books, 1976).

De Roin, Nancy, ed., *Jataka Tales: Fables from the Buddha* (New York: Dell, 1975).

Dickinson, Peter, *City of Gold* (New York: Random House, 1980).

Doherty, Berlie, *Granny Was a Buffer Girl* (London: Lions, 1988).

Downie, Mary Alice, with Mann Hwa Huang-Hui, *The Buffalo boy and the Weaver Girl* (Kingston, Ontario: Quarry Press, 1989).

Edwards, Richard, *The Word Party* (Harmondsworth: Puffin, 1987).

Egan, Kieran, *Teaching as Story Telling* (London, Ontario: The Althouse Press, 1987).

Fields, Julia, *The Green Lion of Zion Street* (New York: Margaret K. McElderry Books, 1988).

Fleischman, Paul, *I Am Phoenix* (New York: Harper & Row, 1985).

Fox, Geoff, and Michael Benton, *Teaching Literature from Nine to Fourteen* (Oxford: Oxford University Press, 1985).

Fox, Mem, *Hattie and the Fox* (New York: Bradbury, 1987).

Fox, Paula, *The One-Eyed Cat* (New York: Dell, 1985).

French, Fiona, *Snow White in New York* (New York: Oxford, 1986).

Fry, Donald, *Children Talk about Books: Seeing Themselves as Readers* (Milton Keynes: Open University Press, 1985).

Fuentes, Carlos, quoted in *People Magazine* (October 14, 1988).

Garfield, Leon, *King Nimrod's Tower* (New York: Lothrop, Lee & Shepard, 1982).

----------, *Smith* (Harmondsworth: Puffin, 1967).

Garner, Allan, "Tom Poker", in *A Bag of Moonshine* (London: Collins, 1986).

Gaun, Jamila, *Three Indian Princesses* (London: Methuen, 1987).

Goble, Paul, *The Buffalo Woman* (New York: Bradbury, 1984).

Grifalconi, Ann, *The Village of Round and Square Houses* (New York: Little, Brown, 1986).

Hamilton, Morse and Emily, *My Name Is Emily* (New York: Greenwilow, 1979).

Harrison, Barbara, and Gregory Maguire, *Innocence and Experience: Essays and Conversations on Children's Literature* (New York: Lothrop, Lee & Shepard, 1987).

Heathcote, Dorothy, "Of These Seeds Becoming", in *Educational Drama for Today's Schools*. R. Baird Shuman, ed. (Metuchen, New Jersey: The Scarecrow Press, 1978).

Hickman, Janet, "Responding and Reflecting", in *Teaching Literature*, by R.D. Walshe et al. (New South Wales: PETA, 1983).

Hill, Janet, "Discovering Books: The Adult's Role", in *Puffin Projects and Primary Schools* (Harmondsworth: Penguin, 1971).

Hogrogian, Nonny, *The Cat Who Loved to Sing* (New York: Knopf, 1988).

Holub, Miroslav, "Napoleon", in *Gangsters, Ghosts and Dragonflies*, by Brian Patten. (London: Piccolo, 1983).

Hopkins, Lee Bennett, *Side by Side* (New York: Simon & Schuster, 1989).

Huck, Charlotte, et al., *Children's Literature in the Elementary School* (New York: Holt Rinehart Winston, 1987).

Hughes, Langston, "Aunt Sue's Stories", in *The Dream Keeper* (New York: Alfred A. Knopf, 1986).

Hughes, Ted, *How the Whale Became and Other Stories* (London: Faber, 1985).

----------, *Tales of the Early World* (London: Faber, 1987).

----------, "Myth and Education", in *Writers, Critics and Children*, edited by Geoff Fox et al. (London: Heinemann, 1976).

huigin, sean, *Monsters He Mumbled* (Willowdale, Ontario: Firefly Books, 1989).

Hunter, Mollie, *Talent Is Not Enough* (London: Harper & Row, 1975).

Hutton, Warwick, *Moses in the Bullrushes* (New York: Atheneum, 1986).

Hyman, Trina Schart, "Little Red Riding Hood", in *Once upon a Time* (New York: Putnam and Sons, 1986).

Ike, Jane Hori, and Baruch Zimmerman, *A Japanese Fairy Tale* (New York: Warner, 1982).

Iser, Wolfgang, *The Act of Reading* (London: Routledge & Kegan Paul, 1978).

Jablow, Alta, *Cassire's Lute* (New York: E.P. Dutton, 1971).

Jacobs, Joseph, quoted in *Touch Magic* by Jane Yolen (New York: Philomel, 1981).

Jam, Teddy, and Eric Beddows, *Night Cars* (Toronto: Groundwood, 1988).

Jeffers, Susan, *Cinderella* (New York: Dial — E.P. Dutton, 1985).

----------, *The Snow Queen* (New York: Dial — E.P. Dutton, 1982).

----------, *Thumbelina* (New York: Dial — E.P. Dutton, 1979).

Johnson, Liz, and Cecily O'Neill, *Dorothy Heathcote: Collected Writings on Education and Drama* (London: Hutchinson, 1984).

Kaye, Geraldine, *Comfort Herself* (London: Andre Deutsch, 1984).

Kellogg, Stephen, *Johnny Appleseed* (New York: William Morrow & Co. Inc., 1988).

----------, *Paul Bunyan* (New York: William Morrow & Co. Inc., 1984).

----------, *Pecos Bill* (New York: William Morrow & Co. Inc., 1986).

Kennedy, Richard, *Collected Stories*. Illustrated by Marcia Jewall. (New York: Harper & Row, 1987).

Keyes, D., *Flowers for Algernon* (New York: Bantam, 1985).

Khalsa, Dayal Kaur, *Tales of a Gambling Grandma* (Montreal: Tundra, 1986).

King-Smith, Dick, *The Sheep Pig* (London: Gollancz Ltd., 1983).

Kipling, Rudyard, *The Jungle Book* (London: Macmillan, 1894).

Kitchen, Bert, *Tenrec's Twigs* (New York: Philomel, 1989).

Knotts, Howard, *Great-Grandfather, the Baby and Me* (New York: Atheneum, 1978).

Koralek, Jenny, *Mabel's Story* (Harmondsworth: Puffin, 1986).

Korbrin, Beverly, *Eveopeners* (Harmondsworth: Penguin, 1988).

Kovalski, Maryann, *The Wheels on the Bus* (Toronto: Kids Can Press, 1986).

Krueger, Kermit, *The Golden Swans*. Illustrated by Ed Young. (London: Collins, 1970).

Leaf, Margaret, *The Eyes of the Dragon*. Illustrated by Ed Young. (New York: Lothrop, Lee & Shepard, 1987).

Lee, Dennis, *Jelly Belly* (Toronto: Macmillan, 1985).

Lewis, Naomi, *Proud Knight, Fair Lady*. Illustrated by Angela Barrett. (London: Hutchinson, 1989).

Little, Jean, *Hey World, Here I Am* (Toronto: Kids Can Press, 1987).

----------, "Invitations to Joy". The Canadian Children's Book Centre Annual Lecture #1, 1988.

Lobel, Arnold, *Frog and Toad* (New York: Harper and Row, 1970).

Lottridge, Celia Barker, *The Name of the Tree*. Illustrated by Ian Wallace. (Toronto: Groundwood, 1989).

Lowbury, Edward, "The Huntsman", in *Poems for Over 10-Year-olds*, by Kit Wright (London: Viking Kestrel, 1984).

Lunn, Janet, *The Root Cellar* (Markham, Ontario: Puffin, 1982).

MacLachlan, Patricia, *Sarah, Plain & Tall*. (New York: Harper and Row, 1985).

Manheim, Ralph, "The Hedge King", in *Grimm's Tales for Young and Old* (New York: Doubleday, 1977).

Mann, Peggy, *My Dad Lives in a Downtown Hotel* (New York: Doubleday, 1973).

Mark, Jan, "William's Verison", in *Nothing to be Afraid of* (London: Viking Kestrel, 1977).

Marshall, James, *George and Martha* (Boston: Houghton Mifflin, 1972).

Martin, Bill Jr., "A Memoir", in *Children's Literature in the Reading Program*, by Bernice Culinan (Newark, Delaware: IRA, 1987).

----------, "Teacher Notes", in *Sounds of Language* (New York: Holt Rinehart Winston, 1970).

Martin, Frances, "Sketco the Raven", in *North American Legends*, by Virginia Haviland (New York: Faber & Faber, 1979).

Martin, Valerie, "Waiting for the Story to Start", in *The New York Times*, February 16, 1988.

Mayne, William, *Kelpie* (London: Jonathan Cape, 1987).

McKissack, Patricia, *Flossie and the Fox* (New York: Dial, 1986).

Meek, Margaret, et al., *The Cool Web: The Pattern of Children's Reading* (London: The Bodley Head, 1977).

----------, "A Time to Wonder", in *Puffin Projects and Primary Schools* (Harmondsworth: Penguin, 1971).

Mikolaycak, Charles, *The Man Who Could Call Down Owls*. (New York: Macmillan, 1984).

Minarik, H. Else, *Little Bear*. Illustrated by Maurice Sendak. (New York: Harper & Row, 1957).

Mole, John, *Boo to a Goose* (Peterborough: Peterloo Poets, 1987).

Montgomery, Ray, *Choose Your Own Adventure* (New York: Dell, 1984).

Morton, Kathryn, "Why Stories Matter", in *New York Times Book Review*, December 23, 1984.

Nesbit, E., *The Story of the Amulet* (london: Puffin, 1906).

Newland, Alan, in *Language Matters*, Numbers 2 and 3. Myra Barrs, ed. (London: Webber Row Teacher's Centre, 1988).

Nicholls, Judith, "Searcher", from "Moses", in *Magic Mirror* (London: Faber & Faber, 1985).

Nimmo, Jenny, *The Snow Spider* (London: Methuen, 1986).

Obed, Ellen Bryan, *Borrowed Black: A Labrador Fantasy* (St. John's, Nfld: Breakwater, 1988).

Ondaatje, Michael, *In the Skin of a Lion* (Toronto: McClelland and Stewart, 1987).

O'Neill, Cecily, "The Wild Things Go to School", in *Drama Contact*. Council of Drama in Education, #12, Autumn 1988.

Opie, Iona and Peter, *Children's Games in Street and Playground* (Oxford: Oxford University Press, 1980).

----------, *The Singing Game* (Oxford: Oxford University Press, 1985).

Opie, Iona, "John Boatman", in *Tail Feathers from Mother Goose* (London: Walker Books Ltd., 1988).

Paterson, Katherine, *Bridge to Terabithia* (New York: Harper and Row, 1977).

----------, *The Crane Wife*. Illustrated by Suekichi Akaba. (New York: Morrow, 1981).

----------, *Gates of Excellence* (New York: E.P. Dutton, 1988).

----------, *The Spying Heart* (New York: E.P. Dutton, 1989).

Paulsen, Gary, *Dogsong* (Harmondsworth: Puffin, 1985).

Perrault, Charles, "Cinderella", in *Perrault's Fairy Tales*. Translated by A.E. Johnson. (New York: Dover, 1969).

Pevear, Richard, *Mister Cat-and-a-half*. Illustrated by Robert Rayevsky (London: Macmillan, 1986).

Pomerantz, Charlotte, *The Chalk Doll*. Illustrated by Frane Lessac (New York: Lippincott, 1989).

Potter, Beatrix, *The Tale of Peter Rabbit* (London: Frederick Warne, 1902).

Protherough, Robert, *Developing Response to Fiction* (Milton Keynes: Open University Press, 1983).

Radice, William, trans., *The Stupid Tiger and Other Tales* (London: Andre Deutsch, 1981).

Reasoner, Charles, *Bringing Children and Books Together* (New York: Dell, 1979).

Reeves, James, "Theseus and the Minotaur", in *Heroes and Monsters: Legends of Ancient Greece* (London: Piccolo, 1987).

Rosen, Betty, *And Noone of It Was Nonsense* (London: Scholastic, 1988).

Rosen, Connie and Harold, *The Language of Primary School Children* (London: Penguin, 1973).

Rosen, Harold, "Postscript", in *And None of It Was Nonsense* (London: Scholastic, 1988).

Rosen, Michael, "Shut Your Mouth When You're Eating", in *Quick, Let's Get Out of Here* (Harmondsworth: Puffin Books, 1985).

Ruben, Hilary, *The Calf of the November Cloud* (London: Piccolo, 1987).

Rylant, Cynthia, *Waiting to Waltz* (New York: Bradbury Press, 1984).

----------, *When I Was Young in the Mountains* (New York: E.P. Dutton, 1982).

San Souci, Robert, *The Enchanted Tapestry* (Toronto: Groundwood, 1988).

Saxby, Maurice, *When John and Judy Don't Read* (New South Wales: PETA, 1978).

Schwartz, Alvin, *Scary Tales to Tell in the Dark* (New York: Harper and Row, 1981).

Scott, Patricia, *Sharing Stories: Storytelling and Reading Aloud* (Tasmania: Piglet Publications, 1979).

Serraillier, Ian, "The Visitor", in *I'll Tell You a Tale* (Harmondsworth: Puffin, 1976).

Sharon, Lois and Bram, *Sharon, Lois and Bram's Mother Goose* (Vancouver: Douglas & McIntyre, 1985).

Silverstein, Shel, "Forgotten Language", in *Where the Sidewalk Ends* (New York: Harper & Row, 1981).

Smith, Frank, *Joining the Literacy Club* (London: Heinemann, 1988).

Snyder, Diane, *The Boy of the Three-Year Nap* (Boston: Houghton Mifflin, 1988).

Stanley, Diane, and Peter Vennema, *Shaka: King of the Zulus* (New York: Morrow, 1988).

Steig, William, *Abel's Island* (New York: Farrar, Straus, 1976).

----------, *Brave Irene* (New York: Farrar, Straus, 1986).

Stones, Rosemary, and Andrew Mann, *Mother Goose Comes to Cable Street* (London: Viking Kestrel, 1977).

Talbot, H., *We're Back!* (New York: Crown, 1988).

Tejima, Keizaburo, *Owl Lake* (New York: Putnam, 1987).

Thomson, Jack, *Understanding Teenagers' Reading* (Sydney: Methuen, 1987).

Tripp, Wallace, *Marguerite, Go Wash Your Feet* (Boston: Houghton Mifflin, 1985).

Tucker, Nicholas, *The Child and the Book* (Cambridge: Cambridge University Press, 1981).

Turner, Ann, *Dakota Dugout* (London: Macmillan, 1985).

----------, *Heron Street* (New York: Harper & Row, 1989).

Waddell, Helen, ''The Woman of the Sea'', in *Folk Tales of the British Isles* by Kevin Crossley-Holland (London: Faber & Faber, 1985).

Wagner, Betty Jane, *Drama as a Learning Medium* (Washington, D.C.: National Education Association, 1976).

Wagner, Jenny, *The Bunyip of Berkeley's Creek*. Illustrated by Ron Brooks (London: Puffin, 1974).

----------, *John Brown, Rose and the Midnight Cat* (Harmondsworth: Puffin, 1980).

Walsh, Jill Paton, *A Parcel of Patterns* (Harmondsworth: Puffin, 1985).

Walshe, R.D., *Teaching Literature* (New South Wales: PETA, 1983).

Wells, Gordon, *The Meaning Makers* (London: Heinemann, 1986).

Westall, Robert, *The Machine-Gunners* (Harmondsworth: Puffin, 1975).

White, E.B., *Charlotte's Webb* (New York: Harper and Row, 1952).

Whitman, Walt, ''The World Below the Brine'', in *The Puffin Book of Salt Sea Verse*, edited by Charles Causley (Harmondsworth: Puffin, 1978).

Williams, Linda, *The Little Old Lady Who Wasn't Afraid of Anything* (New York: Crowell, 1986).

Williams, Vera B. and Jennifer, *Stringbean's Journey to the Sea* (New York: Greenwillow, 1987).

Winter, Jeanette, *The Girl and the Moon Man* (New York: Pantheon, 1984).

Wolkstein, Diane, ''Owl'', in *The Magic Orange Tree* (New York: Schocken Books, 1980).

Wright, Kit, "The Huntsman", in *Poems for Over 10-Year-olds* (Harmondsworth: Puffin, 1984).

Yeoman, John, *The Wild Washerwoman*. Illustrated by Quentin Blake. (London: Hamish Hamilton, 1979).

Yolen, Jane, *Children of the Wolf* (New York: Viking, 1984).

----------, *Favorite Folktales from around the World* (New York: Pantheon, 1986).

----------, *The Girl Who Loved the Wind* (New York: Crowell, 1972).

----------, *Owl Moon*. Illustrated by John Schoenherr. (New York: Philomel, 1987).

----------, "Silent Bianca", in *The Girl Who Cried Flowers* (New York: Crowell, 1974).

----------, *Touch Magic* (New York: Philomel, 1981).

Yorinks, Arthur, *Hey Al* (New York: Farrar, Straus, 1986).

# Index of Authors and Titles

# Publishing Acknowledgments

Every effort has been made to acknowledge all sources of material used in this book. The publishers would be grateful if any errors or omissions were pointed out, so that they may be corrected.

"Our Pond" by Richard Edwards, in *The Word Party* (London: Lutterworth, 1986). "The Huntsman" by Edward Lowbury, in *Poems for Over 10-year-olds* (London: Viking Kestrel, 1984) permission of the author. *17 Kings and 42 Elephants* by Margaret Mahy (New York: Dial, 1987). "Mouth Open, Story Jump Out" and "The Older the Violin the Sweeter the Tune", by John Agard, in *Say It Again, Granny!* (London: The Bodley Head, 1986). "Searcher" by Judith Nicholls, in *Magic Mirror* (London: Faber & Faber, 1985). "Shut Your Mouth When You're Eating" by Michael Rosen, in *Quick, Let's Get Out of Here* (Harmondsworth: Puffin, 1985). "The Big Toe" by Richard Chase, in *American Folk Tales and Songs* (New York: Signet Key Books, 1956). "Aunt Sue's Stories" by Langston Hughes, in *The Dream Keeper and Other Poems* (New York: Alfred A. Knopf, 1986). "Forgotten Language" by Shel Silverstein, in *A Light in the Attic* (New York: Harper & Row, 1981). "Napoleon" by Miroslav Holub, in *Gangsters, Ghosts & Dragonflies* by Brian Patten (London: Piccolo, 1983). "Charity Chadder" by Charles Causley, in *Early in the Morning* (London: Viking Kestrel, 1986). *Dear Mr. Henshaw* by Beverly Cleary (New York: Dell, 1982). *I Am the Cheese* by Robert Cormier (New York: Dell, 1977).

We would also like to thank the Centre for Language in Primary Education, Inner London Educational Authority, for excerpts from *Language Matters*, #2 and #3, 1988; and the Canadian Children's Book Centre, for excerpts from "Invitations to Joy", a speech by Jean Little.